W9-BID-087

GOD DOESN'T PLAY ZONE DEFENSE

Brian,

Loots Luck

God Bless

Jerry Baldwin

Jim Phelan

12/7/12

GOD DOESN'T PLAY ZONE DEFENSE

A PRACTICAL GAME PLAN FOR BUILDING A "1-ON-1" RELATIONSHIP WITH GOD

Jeff Balistrere

WinePressPublishing
Great Books, Defined.

© 2012 by Jeff Balistrere. All rights reserved.

WinePress Publishing (PO Box 428, Enumclaw, WA 98022) functions only as book publisher. As such, the ultimate design, content, editorial accuracy, and views expressed or implied in this work are those of the author.

No part of this publication may be reproduced, stored in a retrieval system, or transmitted in any way by any means—electronic, mechanical, photocopy, recording, or otherwise—without the prior permission of the copyright holder, except as provided by USA copyright law.

Unless otherwise noted, all Scriptures are taken from the *New American Standard Bible*, © 1960, 1963, 1968, 1971, 1972, 1973, 1975, 1977 by The Lockman Foundation. Used by permission.

Hard Cover:
ISBN 13: 978-1-4141-2461-2
ISBN 10: 1-4141-2461-9

Soft Cover:
ISBN 13: 978-1-4141-2309-7
ISBN 10: 1-4141-2309-4

Library of Congress Catalog Card Number: 2012902638

To God, for motivating me to write.

To my amazing wife, Margot, and wonderful children—for their help and encouragement. May we all grow closer to God and to each other every day.

To my mother and father for the many words of wisdom shared in this book, and for their commitment to raise my brother and me close to God—the greatest gift they ever gave us.

To my brother for being the best role model and big brother in the world.

To my spiritual director for encouraging me to write.

To my grandfather and grandmother, "Guma and Gumpa," for teaching me the value of a good day's labor, and for instilling in me a healthy respect for the gentleman's game of golf.

To my grandfather and grandmother, "Nanny and Pap," who opened their house to help others by sharing the gifts of food, friendship, and fellowship, all based in the love of our Lord.

CONTENTS

FOREWORD

"Be strong in body, clean in mind, lofty in ideals."
—James Naismith[1]

DO YOU EVER think back to the sports you played in your youth—in your high school or college days? Do you often find yourself using sports analogies to motivate yourself and to navigate the everyday challenge of life?

If so, then you've picked up the right book.

Between my father, my brother and myself, my family shares a combined fifty years of playing and coaching experience in basketball at all levels except for the NBA. We have found that almost every situation in life can be described with a sports analogy.

As a former Division I scholarship athlete, I had the great honor of playing for Jim Phelan, head coach at Mount St. Mary's University. With 830 victories to his credit, Jim is one of the winningest college basketball coaches of all time. Yet he remains humble, as if he is oblivious to his iconic status in college sports history. He is an even better human being than he is a coach, and I have no doubt that my time on his team made me better at both basketball and life.

The purpose of this book is to bring you the accumulated wisdom that men like Jim have handed down over the years, in an easy-to-read and conversational volume.

I am somewhat of a hard-headed person. I often resist taking criticism or advice from anyone without knowing their credentials and the basis of their authority to speak.

That is part of the reason I don't expect you to take my word for this book's underlying message. It contains words of advice and life lessons from some of basketball's greatest coaches and players. It also includes the lessons I learned from a man I admire more than any of them—my own father. And most importantly, it relies on the Bible, the greatest authority we have. There is no book containing greater wisdom than the divinely-inspired Scriptures. They contain everything you need to know about being truly successful and faithful in life.

God Doesn't Play Zone Defense can and should be shared with children, family, and friends of all ages and walks of life. It is designed to help you build a one-on-one relationship with God. Through the use of sports and the Holy Scriptures, it reminds us that God does not just want some of us to be holy—He wants *all* of us to be holy. He calls us by name. He gives each and every one of us individual attention and intense, personal support throughout our spiritual journey.

Of course, God cannot force us to grow without our cooperation. Our challenge is in cooperating with Him.

In basketball, no amount of natural talent can make a great player. Excellence on the court requires constant practice and sharpening of skills. Likewise, in the spiritual journey, it is always up to each of us to put in the work—to accept God's grace and follow His will for us.

When it comes to our spiritual, family, and professional lives, God blesses us every day with a new opportunity to prep for the big game! Each day we wake up, he asks of us—and we demand of ourselves—a better performance in today's game than we gave in yesterday's. If we apply ourselves consistently, with self-discipline, control, and dedication, we will grow in our personal relationship with God through each season of our lives.

And when we fail, which we will at times, we must not give up, but rather rededicate ourselves to the task. The same attributes that make great athletes are to be found in great husbands, wives, parents, grandparents, sons, and daughters. Most importantly, they make us great sons and daughters of God, and great saints.

As in athletics, this is never easy. The rule of thumb is that if it hurts, it works. But the reward for the pain of hard work and discipline is the championship. The championship we seek in our spiritual life is something far greater than a state title, a Final Four or even a Super Bowl. It is the championship of eternal life with God.

This book is written in the hope that at least one person who has become "lukewarm" in his spiritual life will find in these pages the inspiration and motivation to seek a deeper personal relationship with Jesus, and to draw still more souls to the grace and peace that only He can offer.

So "lace them up tight," "slap the floor and get in your stance," and be "ready from the jump" to enjoy what follows. It is my hope and prayer that it will help you and your family build a one-on-one relationship with God, and to win that most important of all championships: eternal life with God.

CHAPTER 1

YOU ARE THE NUMBER ONE PICK IN THE DRAFT

"Many athletes have tremendous God-given gifts,
but they don't focus on the development of those gifts.
Who are these individuals? You've never heard of
them—and you never will. It's true in sports and it's
true everywhere in life. Hard work is the
difference. Very hard work."
—John Wooden[2]

"POTENTIAL." WHAT A double-edged sword that word can be!

It might be one of the most widely used words in sports to describe young athletes. "You have great potential," people say. But what they're really offering is not so much praise as it is a question—a challenge.

"What are you going to do with all that potential?"

Potential is a wonderful and exciting gift. But for those unwilling to respond, it is a burden. It can even become a source of great disappointment for players who want to avoid putting in the effort, time, and hard work that greatness requires.

Success occurs in sports when great potential—God-given ability—meets great effort. Sports potential is almost never realized through simple luck. As the great golfer, Gary Player, once said, "The harder I work, the luckier I get."[3]

The players with the greatest potential—the number one picks in the NBA draft—receive huge contracts with signing bonuses. They are treated with special care and given all kinds of individual attention—because they are "special." The players who think their "special" status is enough are the ones who go on to disappoint everyone with their unremarkable careers.

A first-round draft pick is not a lottery ticket. It's really a huge responsibility—a challenge, or a series of smaller challenges. Just think of the high expectations and the pressure that falls on every number one NBA draft pick.

In life, we all have the same opportunity—and face the same pressure—as the top NBA draft pick. Just as God blesses athletes with natural talents they did not create themselves, God has blessed us all with many gifts we did nothing to deserve, and all with a goal in mind. His greatest gift is the life of his only Son, which was freely given to save us from our own weakness. From this gift comes our only genuine, long-term reason for constant joy and hope in life.

To illustrate how precious you are to God, read the following sentence and then think about it with your eyes closed. *If you had been the only person when Jesus came to earth, He still would have died on the cross just for you*—just for your sins. That is how special and precious you are to Him. God does not play zone defense, engaging "humanity" as a whole. He engages every man and woman individually. He wants a one-on-one relationship with *you*.

You may have heard that athletic recruiters are scoping out players at younger and younger ages. But God has scoped you out even earlier:

> Before I formed you in the womb I knew you, and before you were born I consecrated you; I have appointed you a prophet to the nations.
>
> —Jeremiah 1:5

God has also given every single one of us another great gift—a free will, with which we can literally do as we please. This beautiful Bible passage, from the Wisdom of Sirach, describes the great meaning of this gift:

> When God, in the beginning, created man, he made him subject to his own free choice.
> If you choose you can keep the commandments; it is loyalty to do his will.
> There are set before you fire and water; to whichever you choose, stretch forth your hand.
> Before man are life and death, whichever he chooses shall be given him.
> Immense is the wisdom of the LORD; he is mighty in power, and all-seeing.
> The eyes of God see all he has made; he understands man's every deed.
> No man does he command to sin, to none does he give strength for lies.
>
> —Sirach 15:14-20

At every moment, we can choose water or fire—to serve God, or to serve ourselves. Our freedom is an incredible gift because with it God makes us like Himself. But the problem with this gift is that we sometimes abuse it. We use our free will selfishly, to pursue earthly pleasures that are poor substitutes for His will and His kingdom.

Regardless of what talents and gifts God has given you, you and every person on earth face the same choice: Will you use your own gifts and potential for God, or for yourself?

For example, those with wealth can use it in different ways. One option they have is to be content with their riches and to ignore God. Jesus told the story of a man who did just that—who said to himself, "You have many goods laid up for many years to come; take your ease, eat, drink and be merry." To which God replied:

> Thou fool, this night thy soul shall be required of thee:
> then whose shall those things be, which thou
> hast provided?
> —Luke 12:20

Given how much people love money, it should come as no surprise that the rich face a great spiritual challenge—a challenge of humility and generosity—to go along with their material well-being. As Jesus taught us, "It is much more difficult for the rich man to obtain heaven" (Matt. 19:23-24).

God did not say a rich man cannot obtain heaven, but only that it is more difficult to be humble and childlike with riches. But with God, anything is possible.

Whatever gifts and challenges that God has given you, He is also your biggest fan and your best coach. He is rooting for you to "win the championship" of eternal life. If we let Him, God uses each of us as His instrument of love, to spread His word and peace through our actions and our words.

God has picked you to be on His team, just as NBA teams choose their top draft picks. Like the top NBA pick, you don't get to choose who drafts you. The Lord has picked you to be a disciple, not vice versa. If you have the passion to follow Him, it is because He has called you.

But you do get to choose whether you will cooperate with God's team or remove your shoes and sit on the sidelines. As with every top NBA draft pick, it is up to you to exercise the discipline, humility, and hard work it takes to succeed.

We have all heard stories about players with great potential who just never panned out. We also know of stories of average, ordinary players whose incredible discipline and work ethic made them great.

Our journey toward eternal life with God is also like the NBA in that "All are welcome but few are chosen." Anyone can play in the NBA—in theory, at least—but very few are drafted or signed. The ones who do make it have put in a lot of hard work to become good enough. We need to take that same approach to our spiritual lives. It is something that requires many hours and daily work to make our souls better, stronger, and more resistant to temptation.

A winner is someone who recognizes his God-given talents, works his tail off to develop them into skills, and uses these skills to accomplish his goals.
—Larry Bird[4]

Jesus Christ once told a story about three servants whose master entrusted them with sums of money ("talents") and then went on a trip. Two of the three realized the value of what they had been given and set out to increase it. They invested the cash and reaped generous returns, delighting their master:

> "Well done, my good and faithful servant. Since you were faithful in small matters, I will give you great responsibilities. Come, share your master's joy."
> —Matthew 25:23

But the third servant was content to bury his money and wait for his master's return. He thought that it would be enough for him to give it back unspent. He was mistaken:

> "Take the talent from him and give it to the one who has ten. For the one who has will be given more, and he will have more than enough. But the one who does not have, even what he has will be taken from him. And throw that worthless slave into the outer darkness, where there will be weeping and gnashing of teeth."
> —Matthew 25:28-30

You have potential. You are the number one pick in the draft. God has given you the ability to be a saint.

But what are you doing with it?

Will you satisfy yourself with the idea that God has given you great value, and stop there? Will you take personal pride in that value, as if you and not God were somehow responsible for it? Or will you apply yourself wholeheartedly, hoping to make the most of all of His gifts?

You will never even maintain, let alone strengthen, your relationship with God with a lazy attitude—a belief that your native talents will make up for your lack of effort. Those around you are depending on you. Just as an NBA team builds a team around a #1 player in the draft, God has picked you so that you can reach out and influence others, spreading His word through your example, and at times through your words.

There is a Latin phrase that millions of pupils of Jesuit schools have learned over the decades: *Ad maiorem Dei gloriam*. It means "For the greater glory of God." Students were directed to write the initials for those words—AMDG—at the top of every paper they wrote, and every test they took. The simple idea is that every piece of work they did—every small thing, every day—was for the greater glory of God.

You don't need to write AMDG on anything, and you don't have to know anything about Jesuits to learn from this concept. Just remember that every task and every moment of every day is an opportunity to offer God our prayers, works, joys, and sufferings—to make all of them serve His greater glory.

There are innumerable examples of how you can do this, and most of them involve enriching the lives of those around you. Think of all the times laziness tempts you to avoid the effort to help and engage others. What if you were to resist the temptation and put forth the effort anyway?

This could mean something as simple as holding the door for someone or saying good morning to a co-worker in the elevator when you're tired and you don't feel like it. It could mean showing genuine interest in your friends—asking them about their families and their favorite hobbies. It could also mean ending a conversation that is harmful to others, as much as you might be tempted to take the easy route of participating in frivolous "water cooler gossip."

When you get home after a hard day's work, perhaps it means engaging your spouse and children in conversation, as much as you would prefer to take a well-deserved rest on your favorite chair, crack open a cold one, and bury yourself in the newspaper.

Challenge yourself to glorify God with these and other small choices you make. If you strive to please Him first, then everything else will follow.

"I told him, 'Son, what is it with you? Is it ignorance or apathy?' He said, 'Coach, I don't know and I don't care.'"
—Former Utah Jazz president Frank Layden, on a former player.[5]

If you spend enough time in basketball circles, you will probably hear coaches talk about two very different types of young players who have "potential." Some of them fall into the category of the "Tuxedo Player." Others are referred to by the less-fancy name of "Mr. Fundamental." Both seem to be good players on the surface, but the difference between them could hardly be greater.

The Tuxedo Player gets his name from the lackadaisical manner in which he plays. It's as if he doesn't want to get his nice clothes dirty on the court. He has amazing God-given ability, and that makes him stand out naturally. But for some reason, he refuses to give 100 percent, 100 percent of the time.

However, the Tuxedo Player already *thinks* he's great, perhaps because of his success at a young age level. Unfortunately, this leads him to cultivate an attitude of disrespect for authority—for his coaches and referees. He shows similar disrespect for his fellow players with his selfish manner of play. At times, he demonstrates more concern about his own statistics than he does for the team or even for winning the game.

When the coach tells him, "There is no I in TEAM"—as many coaches do—the Tuxedo Player might offer the cool, smart-aleck response that "TEAM" does contain an "M" and an "E." His lack of discipline rubs off on his fellow players. At his worst, his bad example creates problems for the coach and for the team's overall cohesion.

That's not the most frustrating thing about the Tuxedo player. The most frustrating thing is that he has *so much potential*. If he were to change his attitude and work harder, he could turn an average team into a league, county, state, or national champion. He doesn't, because he doesn't want to.

Although the Tuxedo Player's natural talent makes him stand out for the time being, a good coach understands that this won't last long. Thanks to his overconfidence in himself, and his lack of discipline, he gradually loses whatever advantage he starts with.

> "The only place that success is before
> work is in the dictionary."
> —John Wooden[6]

"Mr. Fundamental" is a very different kind of player with a very different set of priorities. He gets his name from his focus on the fundamentals of the game, and he doesn't mind getting dirty. He is "scrappy"—the term we use on the court to describe someone who never lets up. What he lacks in natural talent, he makes up for by diving on every loose ball. He is first into the gym and last to leave. He maintains a healthy attitude, encouraging his fellow players.

Because the team is his first concern, and because he is a student of the game, Mr. Fundamental can often serve as a second coach for his peers.

My father once coached just such a player, who was always focused on the team and never himself. He was the sort of kid who would run through a wall for you, then turn around and apologize for damaging the wall—and then run through it again!

One day in practice, my father was running a fast-break drill—three offensive players against two on defense. He turned his head for one moment to answer a question from one of the younger players, when all of a sudden he heard the entire team, in unison, let out a painful "OOOOHHHHH!" as loud as you would ever want to hear. Mr. Fundamental was sprawling on the ground in pain. My father had not seen what happened, so he raced over: "Where did you get hit?"

In true "Mr. Fundamental" fashion, the kid answered in a very high weak voice, "At the foul line."

He had tried to take a charge from the team's 265-pound center, who also happened to be the nose guard on the football team. In the noble service of his team, Mr. Fundamental had taken a shot "below the belt"—and we will leave it at that.

It is important that we all have a daily discussion with ourselves about how we use our potential. In our spiritual lives, are we the "Tuxedo Player" or are we "Mr. Fundamental"?

It is not a coincidence that the kids who resemble "Mr. Fundamental" usually go on to succeed in life—whatever it is they end up doing for a living. Of the Tuxedo Players, on the other hand, many coaches find themselves asking, "What ever happened to that kid?"

Don't make God wonder what ever happened to you.

There is a story about how a pastor had fallen very ill on Christmas Eve and was on his death bed. The pastor from the church across town, who was filling in at the Christmas Eve service, announced from the pulpit, "Your pastor is very sick, and he needs a heart transplant." You could hear a pin drop. The pastor then said "We need one of you to give your heart to save your pastor." Everyone in the crowd began to yell, "Take my heart, Take my heart." The pastor asked for silence, and when the crowd calmed down he said, "The way we will choose is I will drop this feather from this pulpit, and whoever it lands on will have the honor of giving their heart to your pastor." So the pastor dropped the feather, and as the feather slowly floated and drifted down toward the crowd they began to yell again, "Take my heart!" But just before the feather was about to land on someone, he or she gave a slight *puff-puff!* and it floated over the crowd.

This story illustrates that sometimes we might have the potential to do great things, but our "heart" is not always fully committed. No one expects you to give up a vital organ for anyone—pastor, preacher, prince, pope, or president. But the moral of this story is that many of us act like followers of Christ on the outside—and may even consider ourselves such—but in fact our "bark" on His behalf is far more fearsome than our "bite." When the decisive moment comes, if we have not made the necessary effort to get to know Him, we may not be ready to make the sacrifices that discipleship requires.

Don't let this be you. God expects you to put in the effort to know Him, and not just pay Him lip service. All you have to do is open your heart and soul to God. Make sure you are "doing your best, and let God do the rest."

Bible Quotes:

"The hand of the diligent shall bear rule: but the
slothful shall be put to forced labor."
—Proverbs 12:24

"When pride comes, then comes disgrace, but with
humility comes wisdom."
—Proverbs 11:2

"Remembering without ceasing your work of faith,
and labor of love."
—1 Thessalonians 1:3

CHAPTER 2

TAKE IT ONE POSSESSION AT A TIME

"Every man's life lies within the present; for the past is spent and done with, and the future is uncertain."
—Marcus Aurelius[7]

URING MY SENIOR year of college, our team had set a Northeast Conference record for regular season wins with sixteen straight. We had also rolled over our opponent in the first round of the conference championship.

I remember it like it was yesterday, sitting in the locker room before the next game with the guys. We were talking about how great it would be to host a conference championship game and have ESPN on campus. We had only one problem—we still had to beat a team that night that we had beaten twice that year already. That might sound easy, but those who have played and coached a lot in sports understand that it is quite difficult to beat any team three times in a single year.

The mood in the locker room was quite confident prior to the game. Rather than "taking one game at a time," we were looking past the only opponent we really had to worry about at that moment.

The next thing I remember was when we called our second time-out. We were already down 22-4. We battled back throughout the game and cut their lead to two points with fifteen seconds left. We lined up a great shot to tie it up, and we missed.

This loss was a painful but lasting life-lesson.

Great coaches know that there is no point in focusing on a "winning season." They don't encourage players to look past their apparently weaker opponents to the stronger ones they will play later on.

Rather, when discussing the season with their players, the great coaches tell them to take it one game at a time. Or they break it down even further, telling them to take it one possession at a time. After all, a "win" is nothing more than a bunch of successful offensive and defensive possessions. A winning season is nothing more than a bunch of individual wins. Therefore, the player who focuses on winning each loose ball, getting each rebound, and defending or scoring in each possession is already doing everything he can to build a winning season. Anything else is just a distraction.

Every good player learns from his past mistakes, but there is little point in looking too far back at games won or lost and wondering what might have been. Likewise, every player wants to think ahead, but there is little point in daydreaming or worrying about future games and what the season might or might not become by its end.

In order to have great seasons, players need only focus on each and every second they are on the court. If they approach each possession as if it were their last—with all the intensity, intelligence, and focus they have—then they eventually find themselves with winning records and successful seasons. Sometimes they are even rewarded with championships.

It all goes back to a few simple, popular principles about which many self-help books have been written: "One thing at a time." "Baby steps." "Live in the now."

Or as Jesus put it long before the self-help genre became so popular: "Do not worry about tomorrow; for tomorrow will care for itself. Each day has enough trouble of its own" (Matt. 6:34).

God asks us for the same type of focus on and commitment to our daily spiritual lives as great players show on the court—to building and strengthening our one-on-one relationships with God. If you approach each day as a gift from God and if you make a concise effort to make every person with whom you come in contact have a better day as a result of speaking with you, then you are on the right path to living as a disciple of Jesus.

> "Attitudes are contagious ... Is yours worth catching?"
> —Unknown[8]

Each "possession" or interaction throughout the day is a potential stepping-stone to heaven. If our intention is right, and God is at the center of our motivation at each moment, then each second will bring us closer to the ultimate championship of eternal life.

This is such a beautiful and simple way of approaching each day when we get out of bed in the morning. Just as it is important for players not to look too far ahead or back during the basketball season, we must have the discipline to trust in God that the progress we are making toward Him at this moment outweighs anything we have done before and any plans we might have for the future.

The great gift from God of living this way is that we get to start fresh each day, to try and do better than we did yesterday. Doesn't this sound a lot like what we do in sports? With each new game, and with each new possession, the player who missed a critical free-throw earlier is given a chance to redeem himself. When practicing, we revisit our old mistakes only insofar as the memory helps us avoid them in the future.

"What to do with a mistake—recognize it, admit it, learn from it, forget it."
—Dean Smith[9]

There once were two cowboys in the Old West who came across an Indian with his ear to the ground.

They overheard him whispering, "Big white covered wagon. Four brown horses. One man in a red shirt, smoking pipe. One man in a white shirt. Woman in blue dress and blue bonnet."

The two cowboys looked at one another, amazed.

"Wow!" one exclaimed. "You can tell all of that just by putting your ear to the ground?"

"No," the Indian groaned. "They ran me over an hour ago."

Sometimes, with our busy lives, it is difficult to live in the present. We read too much into situations that are, in fact, simple. We draw conclusions where we shouldn't. So remember to see things in the present for what they are and do not jump to conclusions or read too much into a situation. Things are not always what they appear to be.

The two greatest impostors in life are known as "Success" and "Failure." Success, if misunderstood, can make us less humble. It can give us the impression that it came through our own work. It wants us to forget that without God working through us, we cannot do anything.

Failure, on the other hand, often causes us to overreact and perceive things as much worse than they really are. At its worst, failure leads us to despair, when in fact there is always a chance for redemption.

We have a term in basketball for players who look too far back on their mistakes, or who are paralyzed by fear of the future. We call them "pretzels" because they get all wrapped around themselves. They feel deep embarrassment about past errors, but mostly just because they are proud and worry about what other people think. They believe that their mistakes live on in everyone else's minds, as if other people had nothing better to think about. As for the future, they view every opportunity as a pitfall; every chance to win as a risk of losing.

> "I would tell players to relax and never think about
> what's at stake. Just think about the basketball game.
> If you start to think about who is going to win the
> championship, you've lost your focus."
> —Michael Jordan[10]

In contrast, the player who focuses intently on each possession is freed from such silly baggage. He plays with purpose and without fear, focusing on each play without preoccupying himself with the outcome. In doing so, he emphasizes exactly what he must at the most important moment ever—*now*.

It is not easy to live in the now, in basketball or in life. But nothing that is worth doing is easy. The human mind is as powerful as any 6'11", 270-lb. center, but an unfocused mind is like a center who throws his elbows wildly, getting into quick foul trouble and essentially becoming a zero-factor in a game that he should dominate.

We cannot change the past. We cannot know the future. The sooner we recognize this, the sooner we let the grace of God drive our actions, and the sooner we discover His peace.

Every time I find myself losing patience, or wanting success in life to come more quickly, I remember a few words of my father's wisdom, which he shared with me on multiple occasions. When he noticed that I was pressing too hard, he would sometimes leave a note on the breakfast table before school. At other times, he would share a soda with me, and sum up the discussion with a simple but powerful phrase:

"Inch by inch, life's a cinch. Yard by yard, it's really hard."

To help you remain disciplined in your basketball and spiritual lives, it may help you to use a daily reminder or pledge that you can put on your bathroom mirror. Any great player or coach knows that you become great through practice, repetition, and commitment. Below is one way to remind yourself each day to stay focused on what is positive, pure, and good. It may help to carry this in your wallet:

My Daily Commitment

1. I commit to read this every day in the morning and at night as I thank God through prayer for the activities of the day or the day to come.

2. I will allow only God, not my peers, to influence my choices and actions.
3. I firmly believe that with God's help, I can accomplish anything!
4. I choose to be positive and bring joy to everyone I meet today.
5. I will treat my parents, teachers, and friends with the same respect I would like them to treat me.

Personalize your "Daily Commitment" and have it reflect that you are a child of God. Be aware that each day is like the big game, and that each of us must do our best to play it well. A "Daily Commitment" will help this become second nature and get us one step closer to a man-to-man relationship with God and the ultimate championship of eternal life.

"The present is a present."

—Unknown[11]

In the first chapter, I mentioned a parable Jesus told about the talents. It is worth looking closely at what happened to the wise servants who took their master's money and invested it, so that he would receive a good return.

The master said to them: "Well done, good and faithful servant: because thou hast been faithful over a few things, I will place thee over many things" (Matt. 25:23).

Life is all about little things.

Think for a moment about the final judgment. If it helps you, think of yourself at the gates of heaven, with fluffy clouds all around, and God sitting before you at a dais with a gavel in his hand.

Of course, it isn't that important whether heaven actually has gates, or whether there are clouds or harps, or whether God would ever hold a gavel. The important thing is that you will find yourself face to face with Him, and all you will have to show Him is your own life.

At that point, your trophies and newspaper articles won't do you any good. None of your coaches, friends, or aunts and uncles will be there to vouch for how great a person or athlete you were. God probably won't be that interested in the championships you won anyway. He won't ask whether you climbed the highest mountains He made, or how many game-winning jumpers you hit.

What will interest Him are all of the little things. *All of them.* Every small choice you have made. Every good and bad decision. Every time you willfully hurt someone—or helped someone. Every time you blew off your responsibilities or fulfilled them. Every time you repented of some wrong, apologized to God and man, made reparation—or simply hardened your heart against Him and others. Every time you put in the extra effort to do something seemingly insignificant, because you knew it would make a big difference for someone else. And every time you just shrugged and decided it wasn't worth the effort.

God knows your heart by the little things you have done—the little choices you have made. He doesn't need you to commit mass murder to see the evil in your heart. Nor does He need you to die a martyr to see that you are fully committed to Him.

The little things matter—and for most of us, they will be decisive.

As Jesus told us:

"He that is faithful in that which is least, is faithful also in that which is greater: and he that is unjust in that which is little, is unjust also in that which is greater."
—Luke 16:10

At that final judgment, how will God look at you? What will He say?

Every coach will tell you it is the little things that win games. The team that does the most little things right gets the "W." Each pass properly made, each box-out and rebound pulled down, each pick set with precision—each of these can make the difference between a good possession and a fruitless one. Each possession, in turn, can make the difference between a win and a loss.

The same applies to life. So live each day as if you were in front of God—because you are—and mind the little things, because they matter. When you stand before Him at the end, you will be looking at a good friend—at your Father—and you will hear Him say to you, "Son, you played a great game! I am proud of you."

Bible Quotes:

The plans of the diligent lead surely to abundance, but everyone who is hasty comes only to poverty.
—Proverbs 21:5

No discipline seems pleasant at the time, but painful. Later on, however, it produces a harvest of righteousness and peace for those who have been trained by it. Therefore, strengthen your feeble arms and weak knees.
—Hebrews 12:11-13

"Truly I tell you, whatever you did for one of the least
of these brothers and sisters of mine, you did for me."
—Matthew 25:40

For the eyes of the LORD range throughout the
earth to strengthen those whose hearts
are fully committed to him.
—2 Chronicles 16:9

CHAPTER 3

BALANCE THE FLOOR

"The key to success is to keep growing in all areas of life—mental, emotional, spiritual, as well as physical."
—Julius Erving[12]

A PHILOSOPHY PROFESSOR once stood before his class with some items in front of him. When the class began, he picked up a very large, empty mayonnaise jar and proceeded to fill it with rocks, approximately two inches in diameter. He asked the students if the jar was full, and they agreed that it was.

Next, he picked up a box of pebbles and poured them into the jar. The pebbles, of course, rolled into the open areas between the rocks. He then asked the students again if the jar was full. They agreed that it was.

So he picked up a box of sand and poured it into the jar. Of course, the sand filled up everything else. He again asked the students if the jar was full. They responded with a unanimous yes.

The professor then produced a cup of coffee from under the table and proceeded to pour the entire contents into the jar—effectively filling the empty space between the sand. The students laughed.

As the laughter subsided, the professor said, "Now, I want you to recognize that this jar represents your life. The rocks are the important things—your family, your spouse, your health, your children—things that if everything else was lost and only they remained, your life would still be full. The pebbles are the other things that matter, like your job, your house, your car. The sand is everything else—the small stuff.

"If you put the sand into the jar first," he continued, "there is no room for the pebbles or the rocks. The same goes for your life. If you spend all your time and energy on unimportant things, you will never have room for the things that are of true importance and substance. Pay attention to the things that are critical to your happiness. Play with your children. Take time to get medical checkups. Take your partner out on dates or for dancing. There will always be time to go to work, clean the house, give a dinner party, and fix the faucet. Take care of the rocks first, the things that really matter. Set your priorities. The rest is just sand."

At that point, one of the students raised her hand and asked what the coffee represented.

Smiling, the professor replied, "I'm glad you asked. It just goes to show you that no matter how full your life may seem, there's always room for a cup of coffee."

"For where your treasure is,
there your heart will be also."
—Matthew 6:21

That professor was trying to show his students the importance of having priorities. For a basketball coach, the key to winning a championship is very similar. A good coach strives to get all of his players working for the "greater good" or "the win." If he has players with the wrong priorities or with selfish intentions, winning becomes far more difficult—or impossible.

There's nothing more frustrating for a coach than to see players on his team put other, often stupid, goals ahead of winning. The worst has to be when players "freeze each other out" over petty jealousies or disputes. Players who do that are obviously disregarding the greater good. A good coach knows he has to put a stop to it immediately.

"Approach the game with no preset agendas
and you'll probably come away surprised
at your overall efforts."
—Phil Jackson[13]

Equally frustrating, if less outrageous, are the players who want to win, but only in the way that puts their own glory ahead of the team. If they don't score "double figures," these players mope and act like they have had a bad game.

For vain players, and for the average fan who has never played the game, double digit scoring might seem like the most important thing. But a good coach knows that the player who holds the other team's best player to ten points below his average, and who gets seven rebounds, six assists, and three steals, is worth at least fifteen points, whether or not he scores a single basket himself. A player like that has what we call a well-balanced floor game. He's pulling down boards, shutting down the other team's scorer, and dishing it to his own team's shooters. These things are all absolutely necessary for the greater good and for victory, even if they bring less personal acclaim.

"Talent wins games, but teamwork and intelligence win championships."

—Michael Jordan[14]

As Larry Bird once put it, "It doesn't matter who scores the points, it's who can get the ball to the scorer."

Balance is the key to any good basketball player or team. You need balanced scoring, balanced floor spacing, and even need balance when shooting and in all other aspects of the game. A team with great balance also will demonstrate discipline, poise, and patience, which are instrumental in being a championship team.

The importance of balance in basketball might not be obvious to the untrained fan, so let me offer just one example. One of the hardest things for a coach is to teach players the difference between good and bad shots, and to train them to take the good shots while having the discipline and understanding of the game to keep from taking the bad ones. To recognize a good shot from a bad one requires experience, film study, daily practice, and good coaching—but it's worth it. An inexperienced player can't tell the difference between a shot he is likely to make and a shot where he has no chance at all. As a result, he takes numerous low-percentage shots that miss. He might as well be handing the ball over to the other team's point guard.

Only with time and experience can players recognize the difference between good shots and bad ones. The player who understands when he can't score—from that angle, from that distance, over that defender, with his momentum carrying him in the wrong direction—can effectively save multiple possessions for his team in each game. He knows to pass the ball to a teammate, instead of taking a low-percentage shot that will probably miss. This is one small way that a player can help his team, often without getting any statistical credit whatsoever.

You cannot win if you have players who take just any shot in hopes of maximizing their own numbers. Such players disrupt a team's momentum and balance. Nor can you win with players who fail to get back on defense or who monopolize the ball, and who fail to pass to the open man when appropriate. Again, such a lack of prioritization disrupts the delicate balance of a championship team.

This same balance is an important key in a successful spiritual life as well.

Sometimes, in life, we find ourselves living for all the wrong things, or at least putting everything in the wrong order. We judge ourselves and other people by superficialities like money, power, position, and worldly respect. We forget what is really important.

If you recognize yourself in this passage—and you might, even if you're trying to do the right thing—then pray to God for a change of heart. The success of our lives will be determined not by our ability to fulfill our own will with earthly success, but by how well we correspond with His will. And many times, we even get more points for the assists, the hustle, and the shots not taken than we do for putting points on the board that make us look good.

God wants us to have a balanced "floor game" in life. He wants us to have the right priorities. Many think of this as a simple balance between work and personal life, but it actually goes much deeper than that. Life's components are each important in their own way, but the most important thing is to put them in the proper order:

1. God
2. Family
3. School/Work
4. Basketball/Play

These are the priorities of life taught to me by my mother and father when I was young, and I have never found any situation in life that provided reasons to make an exception. All four are good things, of course. But it is very true that you can have "too much of a good thing." We really run into problems when one good thing begins to displace a more important good thing.

When we make decisions with those four priorities in the proper order, we can always have peace with those decisions. Many times when we feel stress and anxiety, we can trace it back to having our priorities out of order. It is not easy to keep our balance with work deadlines and the many, many things that demand our attention twenty-four hours a day, seven days a week. When we find ourselves feeling anxious or stressed, we must step back and take a very hard look at where we are placing our main focus.

Making good decisions in life can sometimes be very similar to the fast-paced up and down game of basketball. You can make a mistake at one end of the floor, but if you keep your head up and hustle back down the court, you can be the hero at the other end. Everyone will make mistakes, but the key to life, as in a basketball game, is that the winner is the person that can recognize a mistake and correct it.

Good coaches notice quickly when things aren't going as planned. Perhaps a team's brilliant set-play is disrupted when a defender tips the first pass. In such situations, you'll hear the coach shout, "RESET! RESET!" Resetting allows you to balance the floor by starting all over again. In order to recognize when things are starting to go wrong in our lives, and we need to reset, we need to evaluate our situations frequently.

And as in basketball, we also have time-outs and breaks in play. A coach who has one player taking "bad shots" or not getting back on defense fixes the balance very quickly by substituting out that player at the earliest opportunity—giving him some "pine time" on the bench. We need to do the same thing in our spiritual lives. When you see one part of your life consuming the others and drawing you further from God, it's time to "make a substitution" with something that brings you closer to Him. This may simply mean coming home from the office sooner, or working less after hours at home. It could mean giving up your favorite show or cutting back on your favorite pastime so that you can spend more time with your children. It may mean making time for church instead of spending leisurely Sunday mornings at home. In tougher cases, this may mean changing your circle of friends entirely.

That is where the examination of conscience comes in. We will look at this in greater detail in later chapters, but the examination of conscience is a nightly accounting of how you fulfilled your duties each day, and where you went wrong. If performed with honesty and care, it can give you perspective on where your priorities really are, removed from the hectic events that crowd your day.

Keeping your priorities in balance is a key component to a healthy and positive life. It may take numerous small acts of self-denial each day to keep our life and priorities in balance, but these acts of self-control build our "spiritual muscle" to defend against greater temptations. If we remember in all of our dealings each day to focus on balance and moderation, we will find the grace of God filling our hearts, souls, and minds, and helping us achieve things that we never dreamed possible.

"Life is like riding a bike. It's impossible to maintain balance while standing still."

—Unknown[15]

As I mentioned in the introduction, I had the opportunity to play for one of the greatest basketball coaches of all time, Coach Jim Phelan. Phelan coached more than a thousand games, with 830 wins. He stands in the top ten winningest college coaches of all time. One of the many things he taught me was life balance and how to keep basketball in perspective after I'd had a bad game.

When I played in high school, I remember that every loss was devastating and frustrating. A bad game could eat at me for days. I would replay every possession in my mind, trying to determine what we could have done better. And this obsession with the past was hurting my game. It was taking my attention away from the challenges at hand.

I remember my freshman year in college at Mount St. Mary's when we had a very tough road loss. We were leading the entire game by three to five points and some critical mistakes down the stretch caused us to lose a game that we clearly should have won. It was a team low in the standings and one of those games early in the year that you just have to win.

The team was really down at the beginning of the next practice, but Coach Phelan knew he needed to get our minds right. We had three games in the next seven days, and we needed to prepare and prepare well.

After a slow and quiet warm-up and stretch, the coach gathered us in to start practice. He said something that was very simple but very profound and it changed the mood of the practice immediately:

"Turn the page."

My first reaction was of confusion. *What do you mean, turn the page?* I thought. *We just lost a game we should have won! We need to understand and correct the mistakes.* That was all correct, but not by focusing on the past.

Coach Phelan was right. We needed to let it go—to "turn the page" and go get those next three games. His ability to stay in the present and keep basketball in perspective allowed the team to move past the loss and focus on the challenges in front of us. It was liberating. We had a great practice and ended up winning the next three in a row.

The ability to keep life in perspective is very important. Nothing is ever as bad—or as good—as it seems. It is important not to get too "high" when things are going well, or to dwell on our successes. It is equally important not to get too "low" when we are having a losing streak. The only consistent thing in life is change. As long as we stay centered and balanced, with God as our top priority, followed by family, work, and then leisure, we will end up living out God's will for us.

Bible Quotes:

> So whether you eat or drink or whatever you do,
> do it all for the glory of God.
> —1 Corinthians 10:31

For by him all things were created, in heaven and on earth, visible and invisible, whether thrones or dominions or rulers or authorities—all things were created through him and for him. And he is before all things, and in him all things hold together.
—Colossians 1:16-17

That we may be mutually encouraged by each other's faith, both yours and mine.
—Romans 1:12

CHAPTER 4

BEEF

"It's not the hours you put in your work that counts,
it's the work you put in the hours."
—Sam Ewing[16]

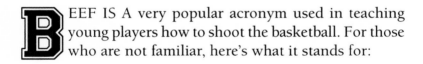EEF IS A very popular acronym used in teaching young players how to shoot the basketball. For those who are not familiar, here's what it stands for:

B—**Balance:** Every good shooter must be balanced and in an athletic stance with feet shoulder-width apart. Your shooting foot (the foot that is the same as your shooting hand) should be slightly in front of your other foot. From this position you are ready to move to the next step in the basketball shot.

E—**Elbow:** The elbow is very key to becoming a great shooter. It must always move evenly within the "slot," or the vertical plane that extends upward from the shooter's side to his temple.

For example, a right-handed shooter would keep his right elbow tight to his side and then raise it up to hold the basketball like a "pizza" ready for delivery right beside his right cheek. At this point, he is perfectly balanced with feet shoulder-width apart, with his shooting foot in front, and with the ball in the "pizza slot" next to his cheek. He could then move to the next step.

E—Eyes: His eyes should always stay fixed on the back of the rim, where he is aiming to shoot. It is very important to stay focused on the rim.

F—Follow-through: This part of the shot is sometimes neglected by the average shooter, but it is very important. When shooting a basketball, you must raise up from the elbow position with your arm up in the air and then do what we call "reach for the peach," "Goose Neck," or perhaps "grab a cookie"—each coach uses a different term for it. They are trying to get their players to picture themselves putting their hand right into the basket as they shoot. The most important thing when following through is to hold the follow-through. Many players shoot, but fail to do this, to the detriment of their technique. Thus, they often miss.

"People who are very good at making excuses are
rarely good at anything else."
—Ben Franklin[17]

BEEF is the method that leads to technically perfect shots. It must be mastered by any player who wants to improve his game. This fundamental process dramatically increases your chances of making a basket, because it causes you to follow the most perfect shooting technique there is.

If you focus on the BEEF process and not the outcome, the outcome will take care of itself.

That all sounds so simple, doesn't it? But mastery of BEEF, like most things in basketball, is a lot more difficult than just learning an acronym. It requires hundreds of hours of practice. It requires thousands of shots, and constant evaluation by good coaches. Only after this arduous process does it become second nature.

As we saw in Chapter 1, God sees great potential in all of us to be saints—His saints, His witnesses, and good examples for others. He can't do much for us unless we give Him the opportunity—that is a consequence of the free will He has given us.

How much effort do you put into cooperating with God's grace? How much time do you spend practicing? Many people think a lot less about reaching this awesome goal than they do about far less important endeavors.

Think of it in terms of math. The average American works forty hours a week, watches television for fourteen hours a week, and goes to church for just one hour a week—if that. Add in a few prayers before meals and bedtime, and you have fewer than two hours a week focused on winning the greatest championship in the universe.

If we look at our lives from an athlete's point of view, we'd come to the same conclusion that many coaches have offered underperforming players who have potential: "You are not putting in enough time practicing."

If you're taking the time to read this book, it's a sign that you probably have the right aspirations for spiritual "stardom." But aspirations are only the beginning. We have to put in time for God, the same way an athlete makes time for practice, no matter how exhausting and tedious it might seem.

Everyone is busy, and so anyone who wants to can come up with one reason or another for why God has to take a back seat in their lives: "I have so many responsibilities with work, with the kids! I coach my daughter's sports team. I have my taxes to do! Dinner to make.... Bills to pay.... Home improvement projects to undertake ..."

My answer to you, as a friend, parent, husband, employee, and also as a youth coach, is that these are all great excuses ... and they're also excuses.

Christ once met a young man who had a better excuse than any of these—his own father had just died. Jesus said: "Follow me, and let the dead bury their dead" (Matt. 8:22).

This instruction was specifically for this one man, whose entire life Jesus knew well. We probably aren't called to neglect our parents' burial. But just think about it for a second—what better excuse could anyone possibly have? Can you seriously suggest that your excuse for neglecting God is better than that man's?

Look at the athlete's example: If something is important enough, you *make time* for it and get it done, in addition to everything else you must do. Basketball players spend hours each day working on BEEF, working on their layups, their rebounding, their dribbling. Is eternal life with God less important to you than fleeting stardom is to them?

If you are really going to do all the things of your day for the greater glory of God, you need to keep sharp and build up "spiritual muscle." You need to pray every day—to talk with Jesus—or else you will find it impossible to recognize Him in the people and situations you encounter each day. Set aside at least fifteen minutes each day—one percent of your day—to spend with Him in silent prayer, to balance your life and find the best way to make it conform to His will. You will find the time if you want to.

If the spiritual life is like the game of basketball, then this is your practice. No player succeeds without constant drilling and strategic planning. Do you think you are any different?

> "Practice doesn't make perfect.
> Perfect practice makes perfect."
> —Vince Lombardi[18]

BEEF, which I explained earlier, is more than just a basketball acronym. We should practice it in our spiritual lives the same way players practice their shots.

How does a funny word like BEEF relate to building a better one-on-one relationship with God? Like this:

Balance—In an earlier chapter, we looked at "balancing the floor" as the key to basketball games, and "balancing our priorities" as a key to life. Part of the so-called "technique" of living a virtuous life requires us to ask ourselves regularly whether our priorities are in the proper order. If you form the habit of asking this question frequently, you can force yourself to recognize when you're going terribly wrong. You might even find that this helps you grow in your relationship with God.

Elbow—It's the pointy part of your arm. Sometimes you use it to prod people. Give yourself such a prod on a regular basis—a nudge or reminder to ask whether your actions are helping or hurting your soul. And don't abuse other people with flagrant elbows, but remember to gently prod your friends and family, to encourage them to stay close to God, utilize their talents to the best of their ability, and help others.

Eyes—Our eyes should remain fixed on Jesus and the cross to avoid being distracted from our relationship with God. As I said in an earlier chapter, don't bog yourself down with distractions, especially when the goal you seek is such an important one—eternal life.

Follow-through—According to the famous saying, 90 percent of life is just showing up. I disagree. The "follow through" is really 100 percent of life.

> "The more you sweat in practice,
>   the less you bleed in battle."
> —Unknown[19]

Jesus once told the story of two brothers, both of whom were asked by their father to work in the field. One said yes, but then changed his mind and decided not to. The other brother refused at first, but later reconsidered. He finally went out and did as his father had asked.

Jesus posed the question: "Which of the two did his father's will?" (Matt. 21:31). That question echoes more good advice that Jesus gave us:

> "Not everyone who says to me, 'Lord, Lord,' will enter
>   the kingdom of heaven, but only the one who does
>   the will of my Father in heaven. Many will say to me
>   on that day, 'Lord, Lord, did we not prophesy in your
>   name? Did we not drive out demons in your name?
>   Did we not do mighty deeds in your name?' Then
>   I will declare to them solemnly, 'I never knew you.
>   Depart from me, you evildoers.'"
> —Matthew 7:21-23

That sounds kind of harsh, doesn't it? But it's really a very simple idea. Anyone can promise to do something, or show up at church, or even read books like this one that try to help with the spiritual life. But the real-life application of a personal relationship with God—the follow-through—is considerably harder.

That's where constant practice and prayer comes in. Each step of this "spiritual BEEF" requires it. Every part of our relationship with God requires it, too.

The poem below is a fantastic example of focusing on the daily process and remaining fixed on God and what is important to lead a successful and giving life.

If you can keep your head when all about you
Are losing theirs and blaming it on you;
If you can trust yourself when all men doubt you,
But make allowance for their doubting too;
If you can wait and not be tired by waiting,
Or, being lied about, don't deal in lies,
Or, being hated, don't give way to hating,
And yet don't look too good, nor talk too wise;
If you can dream—and not make dreams your master;
If you can think—and not make thoughts your aim;
If you can meet with triumph and disaster
And treat those two imposters just the same;
If you can bear to hear the truth you've spoken
Twisted by knaves to make a trap for fools,
Or watch the things you gave your life to broken,

And stoop and build 'em up with worn-out tools;
If you can make one heap of all your winnings
And risk it on one turn of pitch-and-toss,
And lose, and start again at your beginnings
And never breath a word about your loss;
If you can force your heart and nerve and sinew
To serve your turn long after they are gone,
And so hold on when there is nothing in you
Except the will which says to them: "Hold on;"
If you can talk with crowds and keep your virtue,
Or walk with kings—nor lose the common touch;
If neither foes nor loving friends can hurt you;
If all men count with you, but none too much;
If you can fill the unforgiving minute
With sixty seconds' worth of distance run—
Yours is the Earth and everything that's in it,
And—which is more—you'll be a Man my son!

—Rudyard Kipling[20]

Bible Quote:

"For the LORD God is a sun and shield: the LORD will
give grace and glory: no good thing will he withhold
from them that walk uprightly. O LORD of hosts,
blessed is the man that trusteth in thee."

—Psalm 84:11-12

CHAPTER 5

ASSISTS AND TURNOVERS

"We try to stress the little things because little things
lead to big things."
—Steve Alford[21]

I F YOU'VE EVER played the game of basketball at any
level, you'll surely understand the significance of this
poem, by a man named Jeff Smith:

It was only one possession, Why must my coach scream?
My poor defense permitted the basket, But what can one
 hoop mean?
As the pass comes my direction, And I fumble it into the
 stands,
The coach's voice rings loud and clear, "Catch with your
 eyes and hands!"
C'mon, Coach, it's a single possession. Our team will be okay.
It's just the first two minutes, My gosh, we've got all day.

At the ten-minute mark I remember, That the center is strong
and stout.
A putback for two, quite simply due, To my failure to turn
and block out.
But it was only one possession, I didn't commit a crime,
My team is ahead and I'm playing well, And there's still
plenty of time!

As the halftime buzzer is sounding, And I watch the ball
bank in,
I know that I will hear from my loving coach, Of my question-
able effort to defend.
But it was only one possession, Coach—don't have a heart
attack!
We're down by one, but we're having fun, I know we'll get
the lead back!

The second half mirrors the first, But it's early, it's not a big
deal.
That my failure to use a pass fake, Results in an unlikely steal.
But quickly I sink a jumper. I'm greeted by high fives and
slaps,
But next possession I give up a layup, While suffering mental
lapse.
But it's only one possession, C'mon, Coach, chill out.
It's crazy to see you disgusted, As you slap the assistant and
shout.
"Victory favors the team making the fewest mistakes.
Single possessions are the key. So treat them like gold and
do as you're told,
And play with intensity."

I step to the line for one and one, But I have a concentration
lapse.
The ball soars through the air—Good Lord, it's a brick!
I'm afraid the support will collapse. In post-game I sit at my
locker,
Pondering what more I could do. I realize the value of each
possession,
What a shame that we lost by two.

"You can't get much done in life if you only work on
the days when you feel good."
—Jerry West[22]

For a moment, I'd like you to think of this basketball
poem. But as you do so, think of God as the coach, of
yourself as the player, and of life as the game.

We should never sweat over things in life that are
genuinely unimportant. But if you go through life ignoring
the little things—shrugging off important mistakes, without
making any effort to improve—you might find yourself in a
similar situation, realizing only too late that the little things
really do matter.

"Push yourself again and again. Don't give an inch
until the final buzzer sounds."
—Larry Bird[23]

As the poem above teaches us, the little things matter in each and every game of basketball. That's why one of the most important evaluation metrics in basketball is a player's "assist-to-turnover ratio." This number, which casual fans often overlook, provides an accurate reflection of a player's worth on the court. A higher number shows that a player is protecting the basketball and having more positive plays on the court than negative ones. A number less than one suggests a player who is too turnover-prone and could be hurting the team's ability to win.

The definition of an assist in basketball is very straightforward. An assist is the pass that leads to a basket. The assist in basketball might well be the most underrated statistic in all of sports. In hockey, they even keep track of the pass that leads to the pass that leads to the goal. We don't do this in basketball, even though that second-to-last pass before the score is many times the most important one.

A turnover is the opposite of an assist—or more accurately, it is like an assist you give to the other team. Turnovers often lead to easy baskets for the other team. Therefore, in basketball we have this simple, easily-calculated measure of a player's worth that gets beyond the headline stat of points per game.

If we use a statistic like the assist-to-turnover ratio to keep track of the little things in a mere game like basketball, you would expect that we would keep even better tabs on the much bigger question of how we live our own lives. Yet amazingly, if you ask the average Christian how he evaluates himself, you are likely to get a blank stare, or even a look that says: "What, are you crazy?"

In fact, the assist-to-turnover ratio provides a nice analogy to the spiritual life, and one from which we can learn. Assists and turnovers, like most of the things we choose to do each day, are not the flashy, attention-grabbing stuff of a thirty-point performance, or of a flagrant and game-losing technical foul. Yet assists and turnovers are far more common than either of these, and they really do affect the outcomes of games.

The simple fact is that most of us don't perform acts of notorious evil or conspicuous heroism on a daily basis—or perhaps ever. Yet in our daily lives as Christians, we make smaller, less-noticed choices that are just as significant for our souls and for those around us. We try to "assist" others in daily life, which helps to get closer to God and to the final victory of eternal life. We also commit "turnovers" when we sin, handing the ball over to the devil. Our sins set a bad example for others and make it harder for us to win the daily struggle to be a follower of God.

There is a great way to keep track of all the little things each day brings. You can, in fact, keep score in your spiritual life and your relationship with God. It is called an examination of conscience and it is something every serious Christian should do every single night to determine "Was today a stepping stone or stumbling block to the Championship of eternal life with God?"

Here is an example of a brief examination of conscience that you can do to keep your assist-to-turnover ratio in the positive column. Ask the Lord silently at night before bed:

- Lord, what did I do right today?
- What did I do wrong today?
- How could I have done better?
- Did I make good use of my time?
- Did I offer my work to You?
- Did I try and make life pleasant for other people?
- Did I criticize anyone?
- Was I forgiving of others?

- Did I let my body's wants dictate my actions?
- Did I use foul language?
- Did I allow myself to be carried away by pride?
- Did I allow myself to be carried away by sensuality?
- Did I remain humble and give glory to You in my heart for any positive outcomes of the day?

These are just some suggested questions to ask yourself. Perhaps there are others you can add or substitute to make it more your own. The important thing is that you do an examination of conscience every night. And afterward, each night, ask the Lord with sincerity and peace for forgiveness and for the strength to do better tomorrow. Then tell Him, and yourself, that you will work to improve—to:

- Stay away from the temptations you have failed to resist
- Avoid judging others or jumping to conclusions
- Avoid repeating the faults you have shown
- Exert some special effort to improve in a virtue you failed to practice
- Take advantage of any opportunity for improvement

This may be the most important part of all. An examination of conscience is not merely a listing of your mistakes and faults, but also an opportunity to make plans to mend your ways and change your life for the better.

Remember: God has blessed us with free will, and it is up to us to choose to make each interaction in our daily lives an "assist" or "turnover" in His eyes. The examination of conscience is our way of preparing to do so.

Jesus made the point this way: "Be sure of this: if the master of the house had known the hour of night when the thief was coming, he would have stayed awake and not let his house be broken into" (Matt. 24:43-44).

At the end of each day, we have a pretty good idea of our own weaknesses, if we only take time to think about it. Each day, we face certain struggles, and each battle we face represents God's call to us to improve.

> "Me shooting 40 percent at the foul line is just God's way to say nobody's perfect."
> —Shaquille O'Neal[24]

The examination of conscience is our first step toward answering this call. It identifies the areas where we have struggled and must improve. If we fail to examine our consciences, we are simply failing to prepare for tomorrow's struggle, which we know is coming. We become like the homeowner who knows when the robbers are coming, yet does nothing to prepare.

Of course, you're never alone as you study your life and seek to improve it. God is assisting you. He is providing you with the gifts you need to assist both yourself and others.

Anyone who has played with a great point guard or passer who can set up other players to score knows it is a joy. God's help provides us with even greater joy and peace in our lives and in the decisions we make with the guidance of His Holy Spirit.

Bible Quotes:

> "Blessed are they that keep judgment, and he that doeth righteousness at all times."
> —Psalm 106:3

"Children, obey your parents in all things:
for this is well pleasing unto the Lord."
—Colossians 3:20

"He shall call upon me, and I will answer him:
I will be with him in trouble; I will deliver him,
and honour him."
—Psalm 91:15

CHAPTER 6

REBOUND

"It's not whether you get knocked down,
it's whether you get up."
—Vince Lombardi[25]

G OD DOES NOT care who has the most points, assists, or rebounds.

Well, I take that last part back. He does care about rebounds—just not the basketball kind. He cares about our personal rebounds from the sins we commit.

Rebounds are a critical part of basketball. On defense, they are a necessity, because defenders typically have the advantage of inside position—when a defensive team fails to pull down the missed shot, it pays the price, with what is usually two points from an offensive rebound and "put back."

The rebounds we'll discuss in this chapter are more like offensive rebounds than defensive ones. When the offense gets the ball back off the boards, it's a big deal. Suddenly, all the errors that led up to a missed shot are completely forgotten. Your team gets a second chance to score—in effect, a do-over.

The Greek word for "to sin," as it happens, is the same as the word for "to miss"—as in, to miss a target or a basket. When we do evil in God's eyes, we miss the mark. We shoot "bricks" or "airballs." That's where rebounds are so important. No person is free of sin, and not one will find God unless he also finds a way to rebound from his own misses. Luckily, Jesus has us all set up to do so.

The definition of "rebound" in the dictionary is to "come back, catapult with resolve." Note that this definition does not include words like "sulk," "feel sorry for oneself," or "cast blame." To rebound is to be lifted to better and higher places through the recognition and confession of our sins. If we are truly sorry—and the key word there is "truly"—God can and will remove the sin. Through our faith, we can use each experience of falling down as a way of learning to become better people and closer to God.

It is vital to understand that when we sin—especially when we commit grave or mortal sins (breaking of the Ten Commandments)—we reject God. We "box Him out." We conceal from Him any good we have done in the past, so that all He sees is our sin. When the people of Israel sinned against God, the prophet Isaiah wrote:

> "All of us have become like one who is unclean, and
> all our righteous acts are like filthy rags."
> —Isaiah 64:6

I know this may sound harsh and somewhat scary—and it should. When we sin, we deeply offend God. We abuse His great gift of free will. Yet God makes it extraordinarily easy to rebound—far easier than snagging an offensive rebound in basketball.

All we need is to want it, and to ask for it. Jesus has already done the rest by accepting the punishment for our sins on the cross. Just like in rebounding, we just have to want it bad enough to get it.

The moment that we confess our sins and ask for forgiveness, our sin is forgotten and gone. For some Christian denominations, this takes place in a formal, sacramental setting with a priest or minister. For others, confession is a less formal affair. But whatever the tradition in which you practice your Christian faith, confession plays a big role. It lets us show God once again all the good in our souls that has been concealed by our sin. Once again, we are cleansed, and He sees all the wonderful things we do to serve Him.

Even after this miracle, we as human beings may still feel the guilt or disappointment of knowing we sinned. But we must realize that God is right beside us saying, "I FORGIVE YOU."

We all have heard coaches or announcers say, "This game will be won on the boards." That is very true, and it is similar to the game of life. Perhaps you think the saints were perfect people who never made mistakes. The Bible tells a very different story:

> "Though the just man fall seven times,
> he shall rise again ..."
> —Proverbs 24:16

The sign of a strong and faith-filled man or woman is not that he or she is always perfect. No one is perfect. The mark of a saint is his or her ability to get up again after every fall. It is important to ask God's forgiveness and learn from his or her mistakes—to use each one as a catapult to be a better son or daughter to God.

"Failure is not fatal, but failure to change might be."
—John Wooden[26]

The worst player to coach is the one who thinks he knows so much that he can't be taught anything. He won't listen to even the best coach, because he lacks the humility to understand that others have been around longer, and that they might know the game better than he does.

Likewise, when it comes to sin, we don't want to admit we're wrong. We are all in danger of falling to the deadly sin of our Ego and Pride—to hardening our hearts against God. The proud man loves himself too much to admit his faults. He cannot rise up after a fall because, in his blindness, he refuses to admit that he's fallen in the first place.

To be sure, he is aware that he has done wrong at some point, and he might even vaguely admit as much to others, but never in any particular case. Over time, such a man alienates himself from God. The sins harden his heart and reduce his joyfulness and overall happiness in life. With each sin he commits, his sins as a whole become harder for him to admit. As Jesus put it (Luke 6:42), he sees the speck in his brother's eye, but he fails to see the log in his own.

He reacts angrily even to the most constructive, positive criticism. If such a person outwardly professes a belief in Christ, he may dim the view that others hold of Christians in general.

Think carefully for a moment. Do you see even a bit of yourself in that description? We all harbor at least a little bit of that monstrous pride in ourselves. We must always fight it. God will always try to remind us that we are not nearly as wonderful as we think we are. And we must listen:

"If today you hear his voice, harden not your heart …"
—Psalm 95

Stubbornness is not manly. The strongest and most masculine thing a man can do is to admit his weaknesses and failings to God. As St. Francis DeSales once said, "Nothing is so strong as gentleness, and nothing is so gentle as true strength." If we can at least admit our sins and mistakes, then we have two options each time we realize that we have failed God:

1. Punish ourselves and be swallowed up by the feeling of guilt for our sins.
2. Ask for forgiveness, rebound, and become better people and examples of Christ.

That first option is a bad one—another brand of pride called despair. Despair is hopelessness—a tendency to wallow in mistakes without learning from them and moving on. The person who is proud in this way realizes his imperfections, but he utterly fails to reach out for the forgiveness he needs. He thinks he can or should be perfect without God's help. When he inevitably fails, his imperfection throws him into a funk. He indulges in his feelings of self-pity to the point that he is just as incapable of rebounding as the person who won't admit to any wrong.

Do not be this person. Never forget that in basketball good players make mistakes—they blow layups, big leads, and even critical games. It is fine to be upset for a short time over a loss, that is human. But they don't react by feeling sorry for themselves, sulking, or quitting. Rather, they learn from their mistakes. They shake it off and try their hardest not make the same mistake twice.

The ability in basketball to "shake off" a mistake and move on to the next play is crucially important. The game just moves too fast and momentum can shift too quickly to spend time worrying about a play that has already happened. There is nothing you can do about it but make the next play.

> "It's what you get from games you lose that is
> extremely important."
> —Pat Riley[27]

Don't despair. Instead, take the second option and reach out to God. He is ready not only to forgive us, but also to help us turn our weaknesses into strengths.

Think of when you were young and you wanted to strengthen a weakness—for example, to work on dribbling with your weak hand. Perhaps you even practiced for it by eating your cereal with your left hand! I know I did! I am not sure if it worked, but I can go left!

Likewise, whatever your weakness, challenge, or "cross" is in life—whatever difficulty you face that tempts you to sin—you can use it to glorify God. Find it, admit to it, and struggle against it. Offer that struggle to God each day. In that way, you can turn any weakness into a strength. Even if you struggle with serious problems—addictions to alcohol, drugs, or even worse problems—God appreciates all of your efforts. He takes your struggles and helps you become better through them.

Go one-on-one with God. Ask for His help to fix your defects. Luckily for you, God does not play zone defense. He is not just there to save humanity—He is there for you *personally*. No matter how bad you think your own problems are, "with God, all things are possible" (Matt. 19:26).

In a basketball game, just one big rebound can turn the whole game around. This is also the case in life. When we recognize our faults, rebound, and affirm our faith and commitment to be better people and children of God, we can impact hundreds or even thousands more people in a positive way.

Therefore confess your sins to each other and pray for each other so that you may be healed. The prayer of a righteous man is powerful and effective.

—James 5:16

A much loved-minister of God once carried a secret burden of long-past sin deep in his heart. He had committed the sin many years before, during his Bible school training. No one knew what he had done, but they did know he had repented. Even so, he had suffered years of remorse over the incident without feeling any sense of God's forgiveness.

A woman in his church deeply loved God and claimed to have visions in which Jesus Christ spoke to her. The minister, skeptical of her claims, asked her, "The next time you speak to the Lord, would you please ask him what sin your minister committed while he was in Bible school." The woman kindly agreed.

When she came to the church a few days later, the minister asked, "Did He visit you?" She said, "Yes."

"And did you ask Him what sin I committed?"

"Yes, I asked Him," she replied.

"Well, what did He say?"

"He said, 'I don't remember.'"

Sometimes it is harder for us to forgive ourselves than it is for God to forgive us, even when we have repented for our sins. But the miracle and power of confession and forgiveness is that when we confess our sins with true repentance, God immediately takes the weight and burden of sin from us, and as in the story above, he does not even remember it. Our sins disappear, and He again sees the good in us.

Think of it this way: If God doesn't hold this against me, and gives it no weight, what right do I have to give it weight?

And if you are wondering if it may be too late for you to confess your sins to God and you have sinned too much or have been "lukewarm" in your relationship with God, remember again that God does not play zone defense. He is pressing you personally, full court, waiting for you to turn your life over to him.

"If you forgive others their transgressions, your
heavenly Father will forgive you. But if you
do not forgive others, neither will your
Father forgive your transgressions."
—Matthew 6:14-15

In this fictitious story, two long time rival high school coaches, Coach Vincent and Coach McCoy, always seemed to meet in the big game. They did not particularly like one another, and whether it was a summer league game, a scrimmage, a regular season game, or a state championship tournament game, they always found themselves at odds and were constantly at each others' throats. Neither of them would ever give an inch.

After decades of coaching, Coach Vincent died. He arrived at the gates of heaven, and noticed while waiting in line that Saint Peter was asking everyone a question before they could proceed into heaven.

When he reached the front of the queue, Saint Peter said to him, "Hi, Coach Vincent. To see if you qualify for heaven, I need to ask you to spell Jesus for me."

"That's easy," said Coach Vincent. "J-E-S-U-S."

"Great, you're in," Peter replied. "But could you do me a small favor? Take over here for a few minutes; I just need to check on something. I'll be back."

Coach Vincent didn't mind. He took Peter's place and asked everyone in line to spell "Jesus." Just then, old Coach McCoy was coming through the line.

"What are you doing here?" asked old Coach McCoy.

"I am just filling in for Saint Peter," said Coach Vincent. "I have to ask each person to spell one word before they can pass through the gates."

"Oh, yeah? So what's the word?" asked Coach McCoy.

Coach Vincent thought for a moment. "Albuquerque," he said.

This story is just a joke, of course. It's also a reminder. Just as Jesus forgives us for our sins, we must also forgive those who sin against us. In fact, we cannot be forgiven unless we forgive others, and Jesus is very specific about this.

A quick reminder comes to us from the Lord's Prayer: "Forgive us our trespasses, as we forgive those who trespass against us" (Matt. 6:12).

Jesus told a parable that puts our obligation to forgive into perspective. A servant owed his master a huge debt that he could not repay. The master was going to sell him into slavery to pay off the debt, but the servant begged for mercy.

"Moved with compassion," Jesus said, "the master of that servant let him go and forgave him the loan." But the story doesn't end there, since Jesus continues:

"When that servant had left, he found one of his fellow servants who owed him a much smaller amount. He seized him and started to choke him, demanding, 'Pay back what you owe.'

"Falling to his knees, his fellow servant begged him, 'Be patient with me, and I will pay you back.' But he refused. Instead, he had him put in prison until he paid back the debt.

"Now when his fellow servants saw what had happened, they were deeply disturbed, and went to their master and reported the whole affair. His master summoned him and said to him, 'You wicked servant! I forgave you your entire debt because you begged me to. Should you not have had pity on your fellow servant, as I had pity on you?'

"Then in anger his master handed him over to the torturers until he should pay back the whole debt. So will my heavenly Father do to you, unless each of you forgives his brother from his heart."

—Matt. 18:31-35

This is much easier said than done. It takes a lot of faith and strength of character to truly forgive when someone hurts us, but Jesus commands us to do so.

God has forgiven us an enormous debt by forgiving our sins. We are incapable of paying Him back. Remember that when someone commits a far smaller offense against you. Dig deep to forgive—it will catapult your soul and spirit closer to Jesus. It is one small way in which you can imitate God.

Rebounding is critical to winning basketball games. Rebounding in life is critical to winning the game of life, because each of us must have the strength to ask for forgiveness for our human sin, and be aware enough to use our sins as lessons learned and avoid them.

Bible Quotes:

"If we confess our sins, He is faithful and just to
forgive us our sins and to cleanse us
from all unrighteousness."

—1 John 1:9

"'Come now and let us reason together,'
says the Lord, 'though your sins are like scarlet,
they shall be as white as snow.'"

—Isaiah 1:18

Now all the tax collectors and the sinners were coming
near him to listen to him. Both the Pharisees and the
scribes began to grumble, saying, "This man receives
sinners and eats with them."

So he told them this parable, saying, "What man
among you, if he has a hundred sheep and has lost
one of them, does not leave the ninety-nine in the
open pasture and go after the one which is lost
until he finds it?

"When he has found it, he lays it on his
shoulders, rejoicing.

"And when he comes home, he calls together his
friends and his neighbors, saying to them, 'Rejoice
with me, for I have found my sheep which was lost!'

"I tell you that in the same way, there will be more
joy in heaven over one sinner who repents than over
ninety-nine righteous persons who
need no repentance."

—Luke 15:1-7

Then came Peter to him, and said, "Lord, how oft shall
my brother sin against me, and I forgive him?
till seven times?"
Jesus saith unto him, "I say not unto thee, Until seven
times: but, Until seventy times seven."
—Matthew 18:21-22

When I kept silent,
my bones wasted away
through my groaning all day long.
For day and night
your hand was heavy on me;
my strength was sapped
as in the heat of summer.
Then I acknowledged my sin to you
and did not cover up my iniquity.
I said, "I will confess
my transgressions to the LORD."
And you forgave
the guilt of my sin.
Therefore let all the faithful pray to you
while you may be found;
surely the rising of the mighty waters
will not reach them.
You are my hiding place;
you will protect me from trouble
and surround me with songs of deliverance
—Psalm 32:3-7

CHAPTER 7

PROTECT THE PAINT

"It is always better to prepare than repair."
—John C. Maxwell[28]

IN BASKETBALL, "the paint" is a commonly used term for the painted area beneath the basket and between the foul line and baseline. Other words for it are the "key" or the "lane."

On offense, they're setting screens in the paint to free up their teammates to receive passes and take shots. On defense, the goal is to stop all penetration or passes into the "paint." All defenses, zone or man-to-man, are designed to limit the offensive's ability to get into the paint. A successful defensive stand would be a shot taken by the offense that is outside the paint and over an outstretched hand of the defender. Coaches and players will "play the percentages" that this type of shot will be missed more often than not. Over the course of the entire game, an offense will struggle if the defense can keep them out of the paint, reducing them to taking low-percentage shots with hands in their faces.

This is called "protecting the paint." It's the main goal of every defense.

> "I hate it. It looks like a stickup at 7-Eleven. Five guys standing there with their hands in the air."
> —Norm Sloan, on zone defense[29]

The famous saying that the best offense is a good defense contains a great deal of truth. Yes, you can always let your opponent get good looks at the basket, hope that he misses, and collect the rebound if he does. You can always make a comeback after you allow the other team to score. But you can also avoid all of that trouble if you prevent your opponents from getting so much as a decent shot in the first place.

We saw in the last chapter what made the saints unique: they got up again when they fell. The Apostle Peter, for example, denied Christ three times when it mattered most. The Apostle Paul actually persecuted and killed Christians before becoming one of the great saints of the early Church.

So it is crucial to rebound from sin, but there is something even better than a rebound. It is better not to have to rebound.

It is better not to sin in the first place.

The holy men and women mentioned above all have one thing in common. If you could visit heaven for a day and ask any of them about their sins, they would all tell you the same thing: If they could go back and undo all of those sins, they would do so, in a heartbeat. They would do it even if it made their conversion stories far less interesting.

The reason is that sin is an affront to God—an abomination. Small sins are our way of insulting Him with our free will. Serious sins are our way of rejecting Him and His love altogether. And the gravity of sin should remind us, each time we rebound, that God's forgiveness does not come without an obligation on our part to stop sinning—or at least to try.

Jesus taught us a lesson about His forgiveness when the scribes and Pharisees brought before Him a woman who had been caught in the act of adultery, a very serious sin. In an attempt to test Him, they asked whether He approved of stoning her to death, according to the law of Moses.

> Jesus bent down and began to write on the ground with his finger. But when they continued asking him, he straightened up and said to them, "Let the one among you who is without sin be the first to throw a stone at her."
>
> Again he bent down and wrote on the ground.
>
> And in response, they went away one by one, beginning with the elders. So he was left alone with the woman before him.
>
> Then Jesus straightened up and said to her, "Woman, where are they? Has no one condemned you?" She replied, "No one, sir."
>
> Then Jesus said, "Neither do I condemn you. Go, from now on do not sin any more."
>
> —John 8:6-11

Note those last words: "From now on, do not sin any more." This is what Jesus tells us each time that He forgives us. We should take His words seriously each time we rebound, by renewing our intention to avoid all sin in the future.

Sinners, desperately clinging to their favorite sins, keep telling themselves they will do something evil for "one last time." But when it comes to sin, God asks us to make the last time—the previous one, which has already happened—the last time.

> "Some seed fell among thorns, and the thorns
> grew up and choked it."
> —Matthew 13:7

Jesus understands that we all mess up and sin—and He wants us to rebound. He calls us to something better:

> "Be perfect, just as your heavenly Father is perfect."
> —Matthew 5:41

It is a goal we will never fully meet—we are, after all, only human. But we must try and try sincerely each time. God's forgiveness is free, and it's also easy to obtain, and from that we could get the misconception that it's just not a big deal. But it is a *huge* deal. His forgiveness is an enormous gift, given freely and earned for us only by Christ's suffering on the cross.

God's forgiveness should not be taken lightly or presumed upon.

God knows we are human, but he does ask us to strive to be perfect and be saintly. God wants you to be a saint. He calls you to this lofty goal, and He is ready to back you up in any way He can. He is rooting for you more wildly than the craziest student cheering section you can imagine at the biggest championship game ever.

God is your biggest fan. Don't let Him down.

Always think about ways you can improve. The best way to avoid moving backward is to move forward at all times. Improve on your weaknesses. Turn them into strengths. Avoid sin and "near occasions" of sin—temptations you know you will have a hard time resisting.

How many times, when coaching or watching youth basketball, have you said or heard phrases like "dribble with your head up" and "keep your eyes up"? Young players often prefer to watch the ball as they dribble, but this never works. Only a player who is alert to his surroundings can see the defense coming at him, trying to steal the ball or slow down his progress. The player who keeps his head down can easily miss a great opportunity for an easy layup or a quick assist.

We can all agree that being aware and dribbling with one's head up is a simple but important fundamental in the game of basketball. The same is the case in our spiritual lives. We have to watch the whole court and prevent mistakes before they happen. It is a time-tested truth that Jesus himself mentions: When certain relationships or locations or activities present occasions of sin for us, we have to end or avoid them.

But the issue is magnified further still in our modern world of 24/7 media—cell phones, Internet, TV, radio, computers, iPods, iPads, Wii, Xboxes, etc. There are an awful lot of distractions that can keep our heads down if we aren't careful. There are literally hundreds of thousands of images competing for our attention at every moment. It is very important that we are aware of what we ourselves and those around us are taking in.

We need to be aware of and selective about what movies, TV shows, Internet games, and websites that our children are exposed to and habitually watch and use. We need to discuss it with them. And yes, we must also be selective of what we ourselves watch and of what websites we visit. Grown-ups are human, too. Jesus told us that:

> "If your eye causes you to sin, pluck it out. Better for you to enter into the kingdom of God with one eye than with two eyes to be thrown into Gehenna ..."
> —Mark 9:47

Even if He does not mean it literally, Jesus is trying to tell us something important here. Anything that leads us into sin—and there are quite a few things in the digital world that fit this description—we must cut off and cast aside. Today's high-tech world presents the temptations of lust, laziness, and gluttony on a scale man has never known before.

It is not my intent to scare you with this chapter's message, but to ensure that you are aware of the many influences that bombard you each day. Every Christian needs to ask the tough question about what he is allowing in through his eyes: "Is this building up or tearing down my soul?"

Many people may say, "Well, that trashy show, that show that encourages a cynical view of life, that show that degrades my beliefs—that's just entertainment. I know it is not reality, and it does not affect me." Nothing could be further from the truth. Everything you experience and expose yourself to affects your soul. It is up to you to have the self-discipline and control to ask the question of whether a particular form of entertainment is helping or hurting you and your family.

It would be futile and perhaps even counterproductive to go to extremes—to shield yourself or your children from the current culture altogether. But to be a successful family and "protect the paint" in these times, you do need to be radically countercultural. You need to equip your children with the tools to discern which influences are good and which are harmful, and how to resist the latter, even under pressure. The only way to do that is by communicating with your children, empowering them to ask themselves the right question: Is this particular television program, magazine, video game, song, website, etc., building up or tearing down my personal relationship with God?

In the modern culture you will hear objections to this: "You can't shelter your child forever," "If they learn it young, they won't be shocked when they grow older," and other, similar lines of reasoning. There is a kernel of truth to these ideas, but at bottom they are simply wrong. Children should learn the more difficult truths of life from you—not from some crass television show.

Children absorb everything. I once heard a story about a normal seventeen-month-old child, who, to his parents' alarm, started to bob his head up and down constantly. They worried he might have some sort of mental illness. They took him to the doctor, who spent three days testing with CAT scans and blood tests, but found no problems. But in the last meeting before leaving the hospital, the concerned doctor asked what the couple's favorite TV show was, and they responded that it was a heavy metal rock show, featuring the typical frantic head-bobbing known as "head-banging."

Seconds after the parents mentioned this, they burst into tears, quickly realizing that this show had caused his odd behavior. They removed it from their television viewing and within days the head-bobbing stopped.

I beg and urge you to use the television as a teaching tool. Use it to teach your children numbers and the alphabet. Watch a ton of basketball games and films with your children. Watch movies with them that are uplifting and exciting. But do not allow the television to raise your children. This happens all too often. It is destroying our culture and exposing children to things four or five years before age-appropriateness.

"Proactive parenting" helps and empowers our children to have self-discipline and self-control in a "do what I want, when I want society." Peer pressure is very strong, and we must create even stronger-minded children to protect their souls. Protect your children's soul and mind, and they will thank you for it when they are thirty years old and beyond.

This requires a lot of introspection and a healthy spiritual life. As silly as it sounds, people become very, very attached to something as frivolous as a television show – odds are, you know this from experience. The refusal to partake in certain forms of entertainment may earn you or your children funny looks from friends. But unless you do it, you are setting up yourself and your family to have your relationship with God diminished or even suffocated.

Recall the parable Jesus told about the sower, in which the seeds being sown represent the Word of God. Some of the seed falls on rocky ground and never takes root. Some falls on good ground, takes root, and bears great fruit. But some falls among thorns—it takes root, only to be choked off (Matt. 13:5).

What a shame if we voluntarily surround ourselves with thorns, and let God's Word be choked off in our lives.

Jesus tells us to be perfect, but He also reminds us that we seek righteousness—not just the appearance of righteousness, and certainly not self-righteousness. He told his disciples:

"Take care not to perform righteous deeds in order
that people may see them, otherwise, you will have
no recompense from your heavenly Father. When you
give alms, do not blow a trumpet before you, as the
hypocrites do in the synagogues and in the streets to
win the praise of others. Amen, I say to you, they have
received their reward. But when you give alms, do not
let your left hand know what your right is doing, so
that your almsgiving may be secret. And your Father
who sees in secret will repay you."
—Matthew 6:1-4

A great way to live is to do your best and be your best
when no one but God is looking. He is the only true judge
and the only one you have to please. If you follow these
principles each day, God will bless you much more than
you could ever imagine.

It was the most anticipated day of the year at the church.
Saturday, March 20, was the annual three on three basketball
tournament fundraiser and people from all over the town
would come and support the local charities and enjoy a
great day of fun, food, basketball, and fellowship.

The week leading up to this tournament was filled with a
lot of work for the church's men's club. The biggest activity
this year was that the basketball court in the church's back
parking lot needed to be repainted.

Dan was assigned this responsibility. He was always
the guy you turned to if you needed a new set built for the
Christmas or Easter play. If you needed the electricity fixed
in the church hall, Dan could do it. He was truly a "jack of

all trades," and everyone in the church was thankful for his time and commitment to the church.

The week of preparation for the annual basketball tournament began on the prior Sunday with a committee meeting; Dan went to get paint needed for the court. Dan was very particular about keeping costs low, and he felt that two gallons would be enough. Later that week, as Dan began to paint the court, he realized that he was running low on paint. He considered going back to the store to get more, but he had a lot of other things on his plate—fixing the grill, preparing the award tent, and finalizing the speaker system, for starters. So he decided that he would just thin out the paint with a little water and finish the job. No one would know, and it would save him a trip.

When Dan finished, the court really did look fantastic. Everyone said what a wonderful job Dan had done. On Friday morning, the day before the big event, it started to rain. When Dan got to the church at noon, there were about ten people from the committee out at the basketball court, wondering what had happened. The paint in the areas where Dan had thinned it out was completely washed away and half the court was gone.

Dan knew that he had made a mistake in thinning out the paint, but the people of the church had trusted and counted on Dan to make good decisions, and he did not want to admit what he had done. As the committee looked to the heavens, wondering what to do, the dark, raining skies opened and a loud clap of thunder came, followed by a deep, loud voice: "REPAINT and THIN NO MORE!"

At that point, everyone figured out what had happened, and Dan apologized. Later that night he went and got more paint, and the entire committee helped finish the court with just enough time to dry. The tournament was a success and

Dan learned that anything worth doing is worth doing right the first time.

That's how you "protect the paint"—in this case, literally.

Bible Quotes:

> Blessed is the man who does not walk
> in the counsel of the wicked,
> Nor stand in the way of sinners,
> nor sit in company with scoffers.
>
> Rather, the law of the LORD is his joy;
> and on his law he meditates day and night.
> He is like a tree
> planted near streams of water,
> that yields its fruit in season;
> Its leaves never wither;
> whatever he does prospers.
> —Psalm 1:1-3

> "All athletes are disciplined in their training. They do it to win a prize that will fade away, but we do it for an eternal prize. So I run with purpose in every step. I am not just shadowboxing. I discipline my body like an athlete, training it to do what it should. Otherwise, I fear that after preaching to others I myself might be disqualified."
> —1 Corinthians 9:25-27

> "But those who hope in the LORD
> will renew their strength.
> They will soar on wings like eagles;
> they will run and not grow weary,
> they will walk and not be faint."
> —Isaiah 40:31

"We rejoice in our sufferings because we know that
suffering produces perseverance; perseverance,
character; and character, hope."
—Romans 5:3-4

"Peter replied, 'Repent and be baptized, every one of
you, in the name of Jesus Christ for the forgiveness of
your sins. And you will receive the gift
of the Holy Spirit.'"
—Acts 2:38

CHAPTER 8

COACHING MAKES
A GOOD PLAYER GREAT

"Good players can take coaching; great players can
take coaching and learn."
—John Wooden[30]

A HIKER WAS once walking on the edge of the
Grand Canyon on a beautiful summer day. As the
light drew low, and the shadows began to stretch
across the ridges and ledges, he became astounded by the
beauty of the canyon and the colors in the early evening
sky just before sunset.

In fact, he was so distracted by the beauty that he slipped
and fell over the side.

Luckily, as he fell, he was able to grab a branch on the
side of the canyon wall about ten feet below. He yelled at
the top of his lungs, "HELP! Someone! Anyone! Please
save me!"

Just then, the sky opened up and a voice said, "I hear
you, my son. I am with you."

The hiker replied in awe, "God, please save me! What should I do? Tell me! I will do anything!"

God replied, "Just let go of the branch and trust in Me; I will save you."

At that moment the man looked down at the thousand-foot drop, then up again to the ledge ten feet out of his grasp.

He yelled, "IS ANYONE ELSE UP THERE?"

"Plans made with advice succeed;
with wise direction wage your war."
—Proverbs 20:18

This story illustrates that it isn't easy for us to trust—not even to trust God. We stubbornly cling to the idea that we know what's best for ourselves, even when we don't. When things become especially difficult, we start trying to go it alone, at just the moment when we most need clear direction or coaching.

Great basketball players don't create themselves. They have great coaches. Men like John Wooden, Red Auerbach, Phil Jackson, Pat Riley, and Mike Krzyzewski all coached great basketball players and made them even better. And they, too, were all coached or mentored by great coaches at some point.

Great coaches develop great players and great people. If you currently have what you feel is a strong personal relationship with God—or even if you don't and you want to—I suggest you find a Red, a Phil, or a Pat in your church—someone with whom you can sit down and discuss the challenges you face living everyday life as a true Christian.

Be very selective when you choose a "spiritual director/coach." It should be someone striving for the same goals as you, who also desires to strengthen his or her personal relationship with God. This person can be a lay person, priest, deacon, or pastor—but choose wisely, and set aside at least one hour a month to meet with this person to talk about how you are doing in your spiritual journey toward a closer personal relationship with God.

"The next best thing to being wise oneself is to live in a circle of those who are."
—C.S. Lewis[31]

Think about this for a moment in basketball context. Any good player or coach spends hours and hours watching film, replaying every possession of the last game in an effort to try and get better. Division I or NBA coaches have part- or full-time staff to break down and evaluate film and will set aside numerous hours a week to do this. How often do you do it to get better in your spiritual life?

You can start with the brief examination of conscience that we discussed in an earlier chapter. Do that each evening before you go to bed, and honestly ask yourself whether your choices that day brought you closer to or further away from God. And once you're keeping track of your progress in this way, commit to making the data you collect more useful. Bring it to someone who is wise and independent. Provided you are honest and share the untarnished truth to this person in confidence, your spiritual director can provide you with a deeper analysis based on what you've learned about yourself. That is the point of your monthly spiritual "film session" or "team meeting." It can help you see things you are missing as you try to grow in your personal relationship with God.

All Christians profess more or less the same creed. They all have access to the same divinely inspired Scriptures. They all try to live by the same general principles, and that's great.

But as you work to come close to God in your own life, you need someone who understands your particular situation. You need a coach who can see what spiritual skills you should be working on—someone who knows where you are personally strongest and weakest, and what your goals should be at any particular point in time.

You need someone to help you set goals and to follow up with you to see whether you've met them. Otherwise, you might fail to develop as well as you could.

Just like Red, Phil, and Pat, your spiritual coach will ask you to give it your best every day. Like those coaches, he or she will know what you personally need to work on in your particular situation and help you reach your spiritual goals. They will listen and understand when you make mistakes on "the court of life," and help you correct them. They will also give you the requisite kick in the pants when your effort is lacking.

> "If you don't have time to do it right,
> when will you have time to do it over?"
> —John Wooden[32]

It is extremely important to find a pastor, priest, or lay person with whom you can speak freely about your human weaknesses. You will find that it makes you stronger in your relationship with God and other people. Sometimes the hardest thing to do is to be honest with yourself, but having a spiritual director can sometimes help you reach that true honesty much more quickly.

As you go through the spiritual direction process, do not be afraid to go back to basic fundamentals to build your relationship with Jesus. We all know that many times when a basketball team is struggling, that's exactly what it needs—back to basics and *drill, drill, drill* the fundamentals.

"In his heart a man plans his course,
but the Lord directs his steps."
—Proverbs 16:9

You want to go one on one with God. The relationship you seek with Him is very personal. But you still need the help of other people to cultivate that relationship.

We all rely on others. Good players in every sport need good coaches to become great. Likewise, singers need voice coaches, actors need talented directors, students need good teachers and professors, tradesmen begin as apprentices and develop into experienced tradesmen, and so forth.

Even in spiritual matters, we listen to sermons, because we need others to help us understand the gospel. We read spiritual books because their authors help us know more about God and about ourselves. To go back even further, you probably never would have heard of Jesus, had it not been for some person God placed in your life (maybe your parents) to tell you about his Good News.

"It's what you learn, after you know it all, that counts."
—John Wooden[33]

Yes, your relationship with God is a personal one, but it's still one that you never could form properly all on your own. God gave you other good people who can help you become great. Don't fail to take advantage of this blessing.

The famous story of a man named Charles Plumb provides a great illustration of this. Plumb was a Naval aviator in Vietnam who flew seventy-four successful combat missions. His seventy-fifth didn't go so well, though. He was shot down, bailed out, and parachuted safely to the ground. Unfortunately, he was caught and spent the next several years—2,103 days in all—in the brutal captivity of the North Vietnamese communists.

In Chapter 16 of his book *Insights into Excellence*, Plumb writes of an incident that occurred years after he had been freed and returned to the States—after he had received a number of prestigious medals for his heroic service. He was in a restaurant with his wife, when a man he didn't recognize walked over to his table, and exclaimed, "You're Plumb!"

Plumb admitted that yes, he was Charlie Plumb—but how did this man know that? He writes that the man went on:

> "You were on the aircraft carrier Kitty Hawk. You were shot down. You parachuted into enemy hands and spent six years as a prisoner of war."
>
> I said, "How in the world did you know all that?"
> He replied, "Because, I packed your parachute."

Plumb, realizing he owed his life to this man he didn't even recognize, gave him a hearty and grateful embrace. He also couldn't stop thinking about the man. How many times had Plumb crossed paths with him on the boat, without realizing how significant a role he would play in his life?

The lesson is that we are all interconnected. No man is an island, not even as he pursues his strictly personal relationship with God. Jesus gave us the Church, our fellow Christians, and the Scriptures so that we would have help understanding the God we cannot see. We should take full advantage of this by finding a good spiritual director and seeing him or her regularly.

Bible Quotes:

> I will instruct you and teach you in the way you
> should go; I will counsel you with my
> loving eye on you.
> —Psalm 32:8

> The Lord is my shepherd;
> there is nothing I lack.
> In green pastures he makes me lie down;
> to still waters he leads me;
> he restores my soul.
> He guides me along right paths
> for the sake of his name.
> Even though I walk through the valley of the
> shadow of death,
> I will fear no evil, for you are with me;
> your rod and your staff comfort me.
> —Psalm 23:1-4

> And the Lord will guide you continually
> and satisfy your desire in scorched places
> and make your bones strong;
> and you shall be like a watered garden,
> like a spring of water,
> whose waters do not fail.
> —Isaiah 58:12

"Listen to advice and accept instruction, and in the
end you will be wise."
—Proverbs 19:20

"Whoever loves discipline loves knowledge,
but whoever hates reproof is stupid."
—Proverbs 11:1

CHAPTER 9

POISE UNDER PRESSURE

"If you make every game a life and death proposition,
you're going to have problems. For one thing,
you'll be dead a lot."
—Dean Smith[34]

YOU ARE THE coach. You're in the Final Four. Just three seconds left on the clock. You're down two points, and you have the ball. The band is playing. The crowd is roaring.

Your players nervously look at one another in the huddle, wondering what's coming next. What sort of plan do you have? Will it work? When you in-bound the ball, will the first pass go smoothly? Will the right picks be set? Will the shooter succeed, or will he be too nervous to hit the clutch jumper and win?

What is the attribute your team most needs at this moment?

In such a moment of excitement, energy, and intensity, the answer is counterintuitive to what you may think.

You need calm. You need peace.

Every coach wants a team that shows patience and poise under pressure. And every team that has this develops it from a good coach. So as a coach, you need to show tremendous patience and poise for it to rub off on your players.

The single easiest way to gain the most patience and poise in life is to have a personal relationship with God. This isn't just about winning basketball championships, either. If every situation we face daily we offer as service to God, we will have amazing peace with the outcomes, no matter what they are.

As you build your personal relationship with God, you may have people ask you, "How do you remain so calm under pressure?" That is a great opportunity to say, "It is the grace and peace of knowing that God is leading me." This opportunity is ideal for the saying of "preach the gospel and use words when necessary." If we live the gospel then we preach it already with our actions. When given an opportunity to share with people where our equanimity and composure comes from, let them know the truth—that it comes from your one-on-one relationship with God.

There are a number of fantastic spiritual quotes and sayings you can resort to in times of pressure:

- "Let go and let God."
- "God's will, God's way, and God's time."
- The Serenity Prayer: "God grant me the serenity to accept the things I cannot change, the courage to change the things I can, and the wisdom to know the difference."

What an amazing and powerful way to approach life and basketball.

"What then shall we say to this? If God is for us, who can be against us? He who did not spare his own Son but handed him over for us all, how will he not also give us everything else along with him?"
—Romans 8:30-31

There are many things during any basketball game that are out of the players' and coaches' control. In order to play basketball with patience and poise, coaches tell their teams things like "Don't force it," meaning not to make a play or take a shot that is not there. This is the same in life: we need to let God take the lead.

One of the wisest pieces of advice a coach can give is to "Let the game come to you." This means when a good shot or opportunity arises, take it. But do not try to force the issue when the shot isn't there.

"Letting the game come to you" is not the same thing as laziness. It is not acceptable in life or in basketball to say that you'll sit back and do nothing if things are not going your way. You must still hustle and play fantastic defense and rebound. It just means that you need to cool down—to approach things in a calm, collected way that doesn't compromise your chances for success.

It is the same in life. If things are not coming easily, you just need to keep the faith that with hard work, your God-given strength of soul, mind, and body will trump your own impatient desire to get things done your way.

Many times in athletics and business we get confused about who is really doing the work that leads to success. Many times things like pride, ego, and selfishness get in the way of seeing that anything we accomplish in this world is from the grace of God and a true gift. We owe our very existence to God. Everything we accomplish is because of Him—whether the result of the talents He has blessed us with or the situations he has put us in. It is our responsibility to work as hard as we can to make sure that, when the game comes to us, those gifts come forward and bring glory and honor to God.

A great saying that my father used all the time when praying helps us keep our egos in check and give glory to God for our accomplishments:

> "Lord, show me not the way to fortune or fame, or how to win glory and praise to my name but give me the wisdom to tell the great story that Thine is the Kingdom, the Power, and Glory."

When he said this to me, he probably had the first verse of Psalm 115 in mind:

> Not to us, LORD, not to us, but to your
> name give glory.

A great daily exercise to keep us close and connected to God is what is called a "Direction of Intention." This simply means to connect God to as many interactions daily as you can and ask God to help speak through and with you so that the result conforms to His will, and not necessarily to your own short-sighted agenda.

Next time you are on your way to school, practice, a business meeting, family function, or the big game, offer the next hour or two up to God. Ask that He help you understand and accept the outcome, whatever it is. This raises each daily event to God and allows you and your moods to not be affected too much by outcomes. This will help your spiritual, family, and work lives.

If you find yourself worried about the big game, test or business presentation, the greatest relief is to give those worries over to God. The way to do this is simply say: "Lord, I have concerns and constant thoughts about the upcoming event, and it is too much for me to handle alone. I need Your help; I need You to carry some of the burden."

The more we have the discipline to ask God for help, the less stress we will feel in our daily lives.

People often mistakenly view discipline as the opposite of freedom. Freedom, they believe, is simply an ability to do whatever. Discipline, on the other hand, is a form of rigidity.

But, in fact, discipline breeds freedom. The more discipline you have in your life, the more freedom you have. If you can conquer the constant want of worldly things and reach for a higher good, your moods will not be driven by the daily or weekly ups and downs or wins and losses.

This is not to say that a loss does not hurt—it does. But discipline and equanimity allow you to see if for what it is, and prevents it from consuming you. A prayer that may help many coaches and players who are type-A personalities (most athletes and coaches are) is:

> "Lord, give me the strength to control what I can
> control, accept the things I cannot and the
> wisdom to know the difference."

A coach, for example, cannot control every play of a basketball game. He can prepare his team, but the kids need to make the plays. His ability to understand and accept the limits of his power, along with the occasional poor call from the referee, will make him a much better coach. In the same way, your ability to accept your limits will make you a better person in life. The peace and calm that comes with understanding your own powerlessness can truly bring you closer to God.

Mike Sweeny, former major league baseball player and good Christian man, tells a story similar to the one below, related to his career in baseball. I felt the baseball story he tells could also be applied directly to a basketball player's career as well.

Every day when this young boy walked home from school, he daydreamed about two things. One was to play basketball in the NBA. The other was to get a tandem bicycle. Why? Because there was a sticker with a tandem bicycle on his grandfather's Bible, which was kept on the coffee table, and he thought it would be so neat to ride on a two-seated bike.

Every day this boy stopped by the bicycle shop to look at the shiny new bikes in the window, and then went to the playground to play basketball and improve his skills.

This young boy never did get the tandem bike, but he continued to play basketball every day and by the time he was fifteen he was pretty good. During the pickup games every summer evening, the older men would pick this boy first or second for their team, which was a great honor, and as happens on any playground, the best players developed nicknames. This boy's nickname was Tandem, because it took two players to stop him, and other than basketball the only thing he ever talked about was getting a tandem bike.

The boy went on to set records at the high school and play at a Division 1 college. After graduating, he was one of the fortunate ones to have the opportunity to play in the NBA and fulfill one of his dreams. However, only five games into his first NBA season, he hurt his knee badly.

He was released from his team. He began to struggle with self-pity—with the tendency to wonder, "Why me?" He feared he would never have the opportunity to play again.

The young man's grandfather heard of the boy's troubles and arrived at his home one rainy evening about a week after the injury. The young man explained to his grandfather how he did not know what he was going to do—what would his life be like now? Basketball was all he knew. His grandfather opened his rain-drenched overcoat and handed his grandson a gift wrapped in an old flannel shirt that had seen better days.

The young man opened it, and it was the Bible with the tandem bike sticker on it. The young man looked at his wise grandfather, and said, "Grandpa, you know, I always wondered why you had a picture of a tandem bicycle on your Bible, but I did not want to ask."

The grandfather slowly lifted his head, and with a wry smile, he said, "I think now is a good time for you to find out. There is nothing more important than your relationship with the Lord, because one day the 'ball' will stop bouncing. You need to prepare yourself for the championship of eternal life. Everyday this sticker reminds me that my relationship with the Lord is much like riding a tandem bike."

The young man, in his youth, said, "I get it—so God is on the back peddling the bike with me in everything I do. I have known that all my life."

"No," said the grandfather. "There is much more to it than that. The most important thing to understand is who is in the front and who is in the back. You must always let the Lord 'steer' the tandem. You must remember that you are just in the back, peddling your heart out. If you think you can control the bike in any direction you want, you could be in for a big surprise." Because we cannot plan for all situations that arise in our lives. But what we can do is utilize our personal relationship with God to help us peddle through them.

"Tell me about it," said the young man, looking at his knee.

If you try to steer the bike and control every outcome in life, you will eventually crash. But if you can learn from this—if you can resist the pride of placing yourself in front, steering the bike—you will be OK. Peddle for the Lord, and he will guide you to the finish line.

The young man took his grandfather's advice, and his Bible, and used it for motivation to recover from surgery. He did make it back to play in the NBA, and to this day the Bible with the tandem bicycle sticker helps him remember that we cannot control everything and need to put our faith in God and let the Lord steer. But we always need to peddle like crazy with the talents that he has given us, and he will provide the rest.[35]

"Do your best and God will do the rest."
—Unknown[36]

Bible Quotes:

"Therefore do not be anxious about tomorrow,
for tomorrow will be anxious for itself. Let the days
own trouble be sufficient for the day."
—Matthew 6:34

"I will instruct you and teach you in the way you
should go; I will counsel you and watch over you."
—Psalm 32:8

"Be patient and you will finally win, for a soft tongue
can break hard bones."
—Proverbs 28:13

"The steps of a good man are ordered by the Lord."
—Psalm 37:23

"A man's heart plans his way,
but the Lord directs his steps."
—Proverbs 16:9

"The Lord will guide you continually, and satisfy your
needs in parched places, and make your bones
strong, and you shall be like a watered garden,
like a spring of water, whose waters never fail."
—Isaiah 58:11

CHAPTER 10

GOD'S HALL OF FAME

"Champions never complain, they are too
busy getting better."

—Unknown[37]

WHEN I WAS an eight-year-old boy, my whole family took a trip to Springfield, Massachusetts, for a wedding. We did some great perch fishing with my grandfather on an old farm pond with bamboo poles.

My parents also scheduled to visit the Basketball Hall of Fame. But on the way, my father must have taken a wrong turn because we ended up at a park where a group of guys were playing a pickup game.

My father yelled out the window to the teenage group of kids playing ball and said, "Excuse me, does anyone here know how to get to the Basketball Hall of Fame?"

One of the players yelled back, "Practice, man! *Practice*."

Very, very few players ever enter the Basketball Hall of Fame—or any sports hall of fame, for that matter. But it is the greatest honor that any player can receive. Only the players with the greatest natural talents and the strongest desire to be the best in their profession have any chance at all. Even then, they have to be surrounded by the right teammates and coaches who can harness that God-given talent and develop it to the fullest. To make the Hall of Fame, a player must do everything right, and then have all the stars line up properly to boot.

We could say something similar about our spiritual lives, although the parallel is not precise. If we want to get into God's Hall of Fame, we must make the right choices and cultivate the right desires. We need the discipline of daily prayer, church, acts of kindness toward others, self-sacrifice, self-discipline, and constant acts of self-denial. But we have one advantage that even the best players lack. They don't get to choose their teammates and coaches. We do. Beginning in adolescence, we get to decide who will be our friends, our mentors—the people who either lead us toward God, or away from him.

The stakes in our choices could not be greater. Induction into a professional sports Hall of Fame is a great accomplishment on earth, but it pales in comparison to heaven. There is nothing on earth that compares to heaven—nothing at all. Incredibly, anyone can be inducted into God's Hall of Fame. It requires no special talent. Thanks to Jesus' sacrifice on the cross, anyone willing to accept God's grace has access to it, regardless of color, class, or state in life. All are children of God, with an opportunity to choose Him.

But heaven is also … peculiar. Eternal life in heaven is unlike any other goal we have in life because it is a final goal with no others beyond it. When we seek money, knowledge, skill, athletic excellence, and other worthwhile human goals, we do so for the sake of further, future goals. But we do not chase eternal life with God for the sake of anything else—only for its own sake.

And if we lose heaven, there is no consolation game or second-place trophy. There is nothing to be salvaged. This is our only chance in life.

To illustrate this idea to his disciples, Jesus told a short parable: "The kingdom of heaven is like treasure hidden in a field that a man found and hid. In his excitement he went and sold everything he had and bought that field" (Matt. 13:44).

Just imagine this treasure hunter Jesus described— perhaps a poor peasant farmer in the notoriously cruel ancient world. When he found this treasure in the field, he recognized a greater opportunity than he had ever had—perhaps the only opportunity he would ever have for his family's financial stability. If he could only obtain this treasure, his sons would be wealthy men instead of paupers.

And so he sold his house, his plough, his donkey, his shoes, the very clothes off his back. None of those things mattered. Even if he had to walk back to his new plot of land naked—whatever it took to scrape together enough money to buy that land on which the treasure was hidden.

This is what heaven is like—except that heaven is worth far more than any worldly treasure.

"The choices you make in life, make you."
—John Wooden[38]

Many of us spend every waking hour focusing on how we can win the big game, the big contract, the big legal case. And these are all important things, in a relative sense. God did not put us on earth for nothing. He gave us lives to lead, and opportunities to succeed or fail, because He wanted us to be happy in this life. God made the world, and worldly pursuits are only bad when they lead us away from Him.

But it is also easy to lose perspective—to frame our lives not around God, but around worldly accomplishments whose importance is fleeting. It may well be that the temptation to materialism has never been greater than it is today, in our world of cell phones, television, computers, and the Internet. We risk getting distracted and striving to enter the wrong hall of fame—"man's hall of fame."

A great way to approach each day is to picture yourself holding God's hand while "scooping" up the things of this earth—money, fame, good reputation—with your other hand. That is all OK as long as you never let go of God's hand. But the moment you do—the moment you greedily attempt to scoop up worldly things with both hands—you have disconnected yourself from God. And without God as your foundation, you will never earn, make, or win enough in life to be satisfied. In fact, your whole world will be built on a shaky foundation if it's any foundation other than Him. As Jesus put it:

> "I will show you what someone is like who comes to me, listens to my words, and acts on them. That one is like a person building a house, who dug deeply and laid the foundation on rock; when the flood came, the river burst against that house but could not shake it because it had been well built. But the one who listens and does not act is like a person who built a house on the ground without a foundation. When the river burst against it, it collapsed at once and was completely destroyed."
>
> —Luke 6:47-49

The only true satisfaction in life comes from a one-on-one relationship with God. Take a lesson from Saint Augustine, who for years strayed far from God in his quest for worldly pleasures. Augustine later changed his ways and became one of Christ's most ardent followers. He put it well when he wrote, "Our hearts are restless until they rest in You."

Remember that after you die, when you stand before God, your great accomplishments on earth will cease to matter. Your big promotion, the fact that you made partner, the earthly awards of All-State, All-County, MVP, Coach of the Year, valedictorian, Salesman of the Year—you can't take them with you. They will mean nothing.

You will be asked a very simple question, "How do you think you did?" Live your life well, thinking about that final "Team Meeting" with God so that He can look you in the eye, hold out His hand, and say, "Great game. Welcome to God's Hall of Fame!"

Live your life to prepare for this meeting—a meeting with a friend. And say this prayer often on your way: "Lord, show me not the way to fortune or fame, nor how to bring praise and glory to my name, but give me the strength to spread Your great story, that Thine is the kingdom, the power, and glory."

I mentioned earlier that as we strive to reach God's Hall of Fame, we have an advantage that few players receive—the ability to choose our teammates and coaches. As you navigate life daily and continue building a "one-on-one" relationship with God, it is very important to surround yourself with people that have similar life and spiritual goals as you.

I discussed in an earlier chapter how a single player with a bad attitude—a Tuxedo player—can drag down the morale of an entire team. By the same token, we saw that a hard-working player can raise all his teammates' level of play.

Everybody in life is affected—for good or for ill—by the people with whom they surround themselves. You are no different. Friends offer more than just good or bad advice—they also help shape our attitudes and our approaches to life.

My father always encouraged me to seek friends who would bring me closer to God and influence me to do good. A good friend knows how to have a good time, certainly, but he also cares about your mind and your soul. A good friend cares about you for your own sake—and that is Aristotle's definition of love.

And so a good friend looks out for your interests. He understands when you need to study and work instead of staying out. He understands that tomorrow's test is more important than staying up late to watch Gonzaga versus St. Mary's in the midnight game on ESPN. Good friends anchor you and give you balance. They help you stay humble when you are fortunate enough to play a good game.

Good friends make each other better people. Any friendship in which this doesn't happen should be viewed with suspicion.

Bad "friends" and acquaintances can cause a lot of trouble. When you are teetering, they give you a push. They cause otherwise good people to lose their balance. Bad friends may seem fun and exciting in the moment, but this is because they like to pull you away from responsibility and virtue, all for their own amusement.

When you have a good game, a bad friend conveys the devil's temptations to you: *You deserve to relax and party. That test is not such a big deal—you can always make it up.* They are really just disguising themselves as friends, when in fact they are undermining your best interests and making temptations harder for you to resist.

We must be truthful with ourselves regarding the people with whom we surround ourselves. We must be careful about choosing good friends, and we must not hesitate to end "friendships" that are unworthy of the name. True friends make each other better people, but false friends—acquaintances—are anchors that drag us down. They urge us into vices and make us worse human beings.

We must often weigh our friendships—at least on a monthly basis. *Do my day-to-day interactions with this person bringing me closer to God, or further from Him?* We must ask ourselves that now-popular question: "What Would Jesus Do?" Many times we won't like the all-too-obvious answer. But if making the right choices in life were easy, you wouldn't be reading a book on the subject.

None of what I am discussing in this book is easy. But neither are the difficult but necessary things in basketball—the tedious wind sprints and the endless repetition of shooting and ball handling drills so as to perfect the skill to the point that it is all second nature in a game.

Nothing worth doing is easy.

Heaven is the fulfillment of true friendship. It is the full expression of our most important friendship of all—the one-on-one relationship we cultivate with God throughout our lives.

Bible Quotes:

"Physical training is good, but training for godliness
is much better, promising benefits in this
life and in the life to come."
—1 Timothy 4:8

"Whatever you do, work at it with all your heart, as
working for the Lord, not for men, since you know

that you will receive an inheritance from the Lord as a
reward. It is the Lord Christ you are serving."
—Colossians 3:23-24

Set your minds on things that are above,
not on things that are on earth.
—Colossians 3:2

"For the grace of God has appeared, bringing salvation
for all people, training us to renounce ungodliness and
worldly passions, and to live self-controlled, upright,
and godly lives in the present age."
—Titus: 2:11-12

"Anyone who humbles himself will be exulted and
anyone who exults himself will be humbled."
—Matthew 23:12

Jesus answered, "My kingdom is not of this world. If
my kingdom were of this world, my servants would
have been fighting, that I might not be delivered over
to the Jews. But my kingdom is not from the world."
—John 18:36

For any great athlete, coach, writer, musician—or for
anyone in any walk of life—it is very important to set goals
and visualize yourself achieving those goals. The goal of this
book is to be the very last motivational success or self-help
book you should ever need to buy.

"What the mind of man can conceive and believe,
he can achieve."
—Napoleon Hill[39]

I am going to give you the source and secret of everything written in this book, and in every self-help book ever

written. Yes, I know that is a bold statement, but it is true. It all comes from a very popular and powerful book that you may have heard of. It can be found for free in millions of locations.

It is called the Bible. All of the answers to life's questions are there.

If you want to find out the real truth about life and about yourself, I would suggest you begin by reading Proverbs, the Wisdom of Sirach, and the Psalms, from which this book quotes extensively.

You may not always like the answers you find. Sometimes the truth can hurt. We may have an inflated vision of ourselves, of our faith, and of our relationship with God. However, it does not hurt us to be humbled and see the truth. When you read Proverbs, the Wisdom of Sirach, and the Psalms, do not be discouraged or make the excuse that you do not deserve to keep reading because you are guilty. Keep reading!

The truth is valuable and cleansing. As Christ told us, "The truth will set you free." God is a loving and merciful God to those that ask for forgiveness with sincerity. If you need to ask for forgiveness—which all of us should do every day—then ask it with sincerity, move forward, and become a better person.

When you are faced with life's challenges, and you feel overwhelmed, or perhaps you just can't do any more, I suggest you dig deep in your soul and ask yourself whether you've got it backward—whether "perhaps I can't do anything less."

It is a great comfort when you are struggling with anything at home, school, or work to turn your needs over to your one-on-one relationship with God and ask for help. You must remember that you are not just one "of" a million, but you are one "in" a million in the eyes of God. God has called you specifically by name to be his son or daughter, and to bring others closer to him through your word and example. The more we work at developing a one-on-one relationship with God, the more we will feel His grace and peace in our hearts.

The grace and peace we feel in our hearts is a direct result of the work and effort we put into our personal relationship with Him. God always has a plan for us—never forget that He is right there for us when and where we need Him. We just have to reach out.

So if you want a strong relationship with God, it cannot be a soft, sagging zone-defense type of relationship. It needs to be a tight, in your face, one-on-one relationship, and it all starts with you.

Always remember God is calling and reaching out to you one-on-one, because *God Doesn't Play Zone Defense.*

ENDNOTES

1. "James Naismith Quotes." *Thinkexist.com*. Accessed May 7, 2012. http://thinkexist.com/quotation/be-strong-in-body-clean-in-mind-lofty-in-ideals/380174.html.

2. "Basketball Sayings and Basketball Quotes." *Sayings Plus*. Accessed May 7, 2012. http://www.sayingsplus.com/basketball-sayings.html.

3. "The Harder You Work, the Luckier You Get.–Gary Player." *We Are Lucky Earthlings*. Accessed May 7, 2012. http://luckyearthlings.com/oracle/harder-you-work-luckier-you-get-gary-player.

4. "Larry Bird Quotes." *Thinkexist.com*. Accessed May 7, 2012. http://thinkexist.com/quotation/a_winner_is_some-one_who_recognizes_his_god-given/151452.html.

5. "Great Football/Sports Quotes." *Go Mean Green*. Accessed May 7, 2012. http://www.gomeangreen.com/forums/topic/27543-great-footballsports-quotes.

6. "Inspirational Quotes on Running and the Greatest Game of All—Life." *Hoffman's Place*. Accessed May 7, 2012.
http://www.pleasval.k12.ia.us/highschool/teachers/hoffmanjoshua/running_quotes.htm.

7. "'Every Man's Life Lies Within the Present; For the Past Is Spent and Done With, and the Future is Uncertain.' Aurelius, Marcus." *Quotations Book*. Accessed May 7, 2012. http://quotationsbook.com/quote/15185/.

8. "'Attitudes Are Contagious. Is Yours Worth Catching?' by Author Unknown." *Quoteworld.org*. Accessed May 7, 2012.
http://www.quoteworld.org/quotes/10693.

9. "Top 10 List—Famous Basketball Quotes." *Inspirational-Quotes-and-Quotations.com*. Accessed May 7, 2012. http://www.inspirational-quotes-and-quotations.com/famous-basketball-quotes.html.

10. "Basketball Quotes." *Quotes Motivational*. Accessed May 7, 2012.
http://quotes-motivational.com/Motivational/Basketball-Quotes.html.

11. "The Present Quotes." *Thinkexist.com*. Accessed May 7, 2012.
http://thinkexist.com/quotations/the_present/2.html.

12. "Basketball Inspirational and Motivational Quote." *Youth Basketball Tips*. Accessed May 7, 2012.
http://www.youth-basketball-tips.com/inspirational-quote.html.

13. "Phil Jackson Quotes." *Thinkexist.com*. Accessed May 7, 2012.
http://thinkexist.com/quotation/approach_the_game_with_no_preset_agendas_and_you/151339.html.

14. "Michael Jordan Quotes." *Thinkexist.com.* Accessed May 7, 2012. http://thinkexist.com/quotation/talent_wins_games-but_teamwork_and_intelligence/150227.html.

15. *Motivational Stories, Quotes, and Statements.* Accessed May 7, 2012. http://www.basketballsbest.com/motivation5.htm.

16. "Quotation Details." *Quotations Page.* Accessed May 7, 2012. http://www.quotationspage.com/quote/25941.html.

17. "Some Quotes." *English Forums.* Accessed May 7, 2012. http://www.englishforums.com/English/SomeQuotes/wrvjv/post.htm.

18. "'Practice Does Not Make Perfect. Perfect Practice Makes Perfect.' Lombardi, Vince." *Quotations Book.* Accessed May 7, 2012. http://quotationsbook.com/quote/31796/.

19. "Quotations About Sports." *Quote Garden.* Accessed May 7, 2012. http://www.quotegarden.com/sports.html.

20. "Archive of Classic Poems." *Everypoet.com.* Accessed May 7, 2012. http://www.everypoet.com/archive/poetry/Rudyard_Kipling/kipling_if.htm.

21. www.basketball.org. http://www.basketball.org/drills/two-man-shooting/. Accessed June 19, 2012.

22. "Jerry West Quote." *Great-Quotes.com.* Accessed May 7, 2012. http://www.great-quotes.com/quote/705600.

23. "'Push Yourself Again and Again. Don't Give an Inch Until the Final Buzzer Sounds.' Bird, Larry." *Quotations Book.* Accessed May 7, 2012. http://quotationsbook.com/quote/12068/.

24. "Famous Basketball Quotes." *Great-Quotes.com.* Accessed May 7, 2012. http://www.great-quotes.com/Famous_Basketball_Quotes.htm.

25. "Vince Lombardi Quotes." *Thinkexist.com.* Accessed May 7, 2012. http://thinkexist.com/quotation/it-s_not_whether_you_get_knocked_down-it-s/15117.html.

26. "'Failure Is Not Fatal, but Failure to Change Might Be.' Wooden, John." *Quotations Book.* Accessed May 7, 2012. http://quotationsbook.com/quote/13891/.

27. "Famous Basketball Quotes." *Great-Quotes.com.* Accessed May 7, 2012. http://www.great-quotes.com/Famous_Basketball_Quotes.htm.

28. "Planning." *Epictrek.com.* Accessed May 7, 2012. http://epictrek.com/Epictrek/PlanningQuotes.html.

29. "Basketball Quotes, Funny Basketball Quotes, Sayings, Quotations." *All Great Quotes.* Accessed May 7, 2012. http://www.allgreatquotes.com/basketball_quotes2.shtml.

30. "Basketball Coaching Quotes." *CoachLikeaPro.com.* Accessed May 7, 2012. http://www.coachlikeapro.com/basketball-coaching-quotes.html.

31. "C.S. Lewis Quotes." *Thinkexist.com.* Accessed May 7, 2012. http://thinkexist.com/quotation/the_next_best_thing_to_being_wise_oneself_is_to/179310.html.

32. "John Wooden Quotes." *Thinkexist.com.* Accessed May 7, 2012. http://thinkexist.com/quotation/if_you_don-t_have_time_to_do_it_right-when_will/148160.html.

33. "John Wooden Quotes." *Brainy Quote*. Accessed May 7, 2012.
http://www.brainyquote.com/quotes/authors/j/john_wooden.html.

34. "If You Make Every Game a Life and Death Proposition, You're Going to Have Problems. For One Thing, You'll Be Dead a Lot. Dean Smith." *Quoting Quotes*. Accessed May 7, 2012.
http://quotingquotes.com/59874/.

35. Sweeny, Mike. *5-time Major League All-Star on Winning the Game with Christ*. Lighthouse Catholic Media CD.

36. "Do Your Best and God Will Do the Rest." *SermonCentral. com*. Accessed May 7, 2012.
http://www.sermoncentral.com/sermons/do-your-best-and-god-will-do-the-rest-wayne-burnett-sermon-on-what-is-evangelism-33068.asp.

37. "Educational and Motivational Quotes for Your Basketball Team." *Coachlohoops.homestead.com*. Accessed May 7, 2012.
http://coachlokhoops.homestead.com/quotesUntitled1.html.

38. *Coaching Basketball Online*. Accessed May 7, 2012.
http://www.coachingbasketballonline.com/storage/Coach%20Woodenisms%2099%20bday.doc.

39. "'What the Mind of Man can Conceive and Believe, It can Achieve.'—Napoleon Hill." *Quoteworld.org*. Accessed May 7, 2012.
http://www.quoteworld.org/quotes/6574.

WinePressPublishing
Great Books, Defined.

To order additional copies of this book call:
1-877-421-READ (7323)
or please visit our website at
www.WinePressbooks.com

If you enjoyed this quality custom-published book,
drop by our website for more books and information.

www.winepresspublishing.com
"Your partner in custom publishing."

(www.goddoesntplayzonedefense.com)

CPSIA information can be obtained at www.ICGtesting.com
Printed in the USA
BVOW031144041212

307201BV00001B/8/P